I bow before the Great Oneness

Table of Contents

Prophetic Word: I see men coming in procession... each bearing heavy baggage. *One has a duffle bag over his shoulder, full of offerings and things to give up. Another man pushes a heavy metal cart full of large water jugs. There is another who sits on the dusty ground and goes into trance. Behind closed eyes he is told to bring his infant son; three hours later he wakes and tells the others. In the wilderness, a powerful light bursts through the hard dry earth. Divine Presence. The man lays his baby boy on the ground at the feet of this fiery face of God.*

The vision was clear: God is calling Abrahams now. Men who love God and live to do His will are called to submit to the truth and support the work. This truth will bless such men, allowing them to move in grace because they give of themselves to God's chosen wives. Basileia ton Ouranon.[a] The Kingdom is a Queendom.

Ugra Kali Tara isn't the first deity I would've thought to relate to the God of the Bible. Yet during this dream vision, received in 2021, I woke knowing this is the aspect of God which calls for the sons of men. And it makes sense, doesn't it? The notorious image of Mother Kali carrying swords, bearing a bloody garland of male heads, wearing their severed arms around her waist. She renders them immobile– no more doing what has been done. She takes their heads, rendering them free from former thought processes. It's a major waking up… for all of us.

---

[a] Basileia ton Ouranon: One of the original ways of writing "Kingdom of God/Kingdom of heaven" in the bible, see the Gospel of Matthew. From the Greek: Βασιλεία τῶν Ουρανῶν. Basileia is, however, a way to designate "queen" not king. See "The Cult of Divine Birth in Ancient

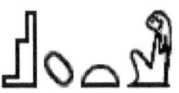

Aset Throne of God
Kemetic/Ancient Egyptian

Greece" by Marguerite Rigoglioso (pg 46-50). *The Basilinna as Holy Parthenos:* "...*The title basileus derived from basile, a queen's title–and name of a goddess–that dated back to the pre-Mycenaean period. The linguistic precedence of the female title basile indicates that the female who held this office stood higher than the king. Thus, the term basilinna was in fact an unnecessary and later feminization of basileus, one that indicates that the basile/queen's status was probably diminished under patriarchy. It is very likely, then, that the ritual of the basilinna originated under matriarchal conditions when she was called the basile.* So basileia ton ouranon gives us "queendom of heaven" and the related phrase, basileia tou theou, gives us "queendom of god." Either way, the rulership denoted is feminine in functionality.

Introduction

Everything born of man dies. That's the whole of this prophetic message in one fell swoop. That's everything. Such a basic and obvious premise, staring us all in the face… for millenia. Hidden in secret societies and mystery schools, biblical innuendo and classical myth. Yet it is the most fundamental truth– comprising the core operating system of our reality. Shouldn't everyone know it?

These assertions are not the fruit of years of scholarly research. I have not studied all the texts of all of the academics who ever tried to piece together "the mysteries." I found that I myself am part of the mystery. As a womb carrier, and (according to the late and esteemed Mama Zogbe via divination) "a true mamissi," these truths are in my blood and in my cellular memory. These mysteries came to be known through direct revelation.

How so? Through dreams, whispers, and yes, there have also been plenty of textual pointings. I've read my share of books to research the revelations. If you've been drawn to this work, you likely have similar mysteries in your blood. Your intuition is keyed in, turned on, and you're seeing synchronicities everywhere. You just know things. That's the type of sister this is written for. You who naturally read between the lines and trust your intuition more than any dogmatic religious text, priests, or what have you. I'm not here to convince you of anything. My job, my calling, is to open my mouth and speak the truth to those with ears to hear.

So what exactly does it mean to be born of man? Afterall, men don't give birth. They don't have wombs. So what on earth am I talking about? Well, men DO have wombs… when women marry them or lie with them and open themselves to penetration by phallus and impregnation by sperm. Men get a womb by proxy– we loan it to them. It's the only way they can perpetuate their gender, by borrowing a woman's womb. And it's the only way we, womb carriers, can procreate when we lose knowledge of *divine conception* with God.

> *"Men are attracted to your woman's spirituality,*
> *your closeness to and ability to manifest God. You*
> *must manifest God, you must make the offerings."*
> *~ Direct revelation via dreamtime*

Although I carry a dusty expired membership card to the I-hate-men club myself, after enduring abusive relationships with males, I cringe at the thought of any extremist "man-hating feminists" running with this, taking it to very dark places. Persecution won't help. On the flip side, certain males might refute this truth out of some sense of being attacked then attack it as a knee jerk reaction. But rest assured, this isn't about hating men. Men have helped us preserve and perpetuate our species when we forgot how to do so according to divine blueprint. Most men I know have been diligent in supporting and protecting the females they love, while of course there have always been other men who do the opposite. Either way, this isn't about going batnuts and hunting them down to tar and feather. So no matter how you take this work, know that such meanness is not my intent. That would be to mimic the abuse and trauma inflicted on women by the more brutal patriarchal forces throughout the ages. This is not about payback or malice.

What it is about is establishing the truth of *divine conception* as a natural way of life on our planet.

Everything born of man dies. To remedy this, we are being called to seek and to reestablish Mother Isis/Aset's mystery schools. She is the mother of God, theotokos. The work of divine birth is our panacea. The heiros gamos temple takeover through heterosexual reproduction must end, where God's professed nuns are concerned. If humanity is to flourish, we must turn to the ways of *divine conception*, establishing temples of Aset the world over. We must create spaces dedicated to this work, spaces where women– and those who identify with or simply support us– can reach for the divine and bring it down to Earth. As priestesses, it is our job to know the Spirit of place, the Spirit of lineage, and to propitiate the Great Holy Spirit of many names and nameless– Ruach HaKodesh.

> *Revelation 22 - Eden Restored:*
>
> *Then the angel showed me the river of the water of life, as clear as crystal, flowing from the **throne of God** and of the Lamb down the middle of the great street of the city. On each side of the river stood the tree of life, bearing twelve crops of fruit, yielding its fruit every month. And the leaves of the tree are for the healing of the nations. No longer will there be any curse. The throne of God and of the Lamb will be in the city, and his servants will serve him. They will see his face, and his name will be on their foreheads. There will be no more night. They will not need the light of a lamp or the light of the sun, for the Lord God will give them light. And they will reign for ever and ever.*

We are on the verge of a new age of Isis.
Throne of IAH ASR IAH. YAHUAH.

As I write this, the rain is falling in quaint Greenbelt Maryland. In lieu of Starbucks (in the time of quarantine) I'm sitting outside the New Deal Cafe, a cozy local coffee shop, named in honor of President Roosevelt's efforts to improve American life in the 1930's. He's responsible for the establishment of this community, with its housing cooperative and centralized amenities. When I first moved here some years ago I dreamt of President Roosevelt's wife, Eleanor. She said, "No more secret wars."

Recently I felt her handprint on the place when I saw a t-shirt for sale at the Co-Op Market which read, "Eleanor Roosevelt High School - Raiders." Above the shirt a sign read, "Spirit Wear." From this my mind clearly received, "Eleanor Roosevelt Spirit." It was a nudge to pay attention-- the "spirit" was present. To the uninitiated or unfamiliar this may seem like nonsense at best or perhaps a schizophrenic delusion at worst. But in various cultures the shaman is notorious for walking a fine line between insanity and sanity... and blurring it.

So, after seeing and registering this message about Eleanor Roosevelt's spirit, a dear student and I walked to the lake, aka Buddy Attick Lake Park. Once there, a man approached us as we sat on a bench overlooking the water. "Do you know the history of this place?" the older white man asked. I mentioned that I knew one of the pioneer families very well, but that we loved a good story. He went on to elucidate, "Eleanore Roosevelt cared about people. She visited a coal mining town in Virginia with her husband, before he was elected president, and while there she

11

saw that people were drinking water from the same river in which they washed their clothes." Our faces scrunched in horror, which he no doubt anticipated. "The people were very poor there. Elenor vowed to return one day and help the community and that's exactly what she did. And you know, she was as influential here. They tried to name the high school after her husband, but the people fought to name it after her!" In my intuitive heart I heard and knew, "She's the mother of this place."

Every place has a spirit. Shinto, Ifa, Bon, Druid, Kardecism, Sangoma, Kemetic Neterianism, and other shamanic traditions have told us so. Traditional religious practitioners from around the world have beat the drum of ancestor reverence since time immemorial-- Lighting candles, burning incense, dancing masquerades. Why? Because mystic practitioners know very well that the dead are not dead.

We honor the elevated ancestors because they've proved themselves to be deserving. They lived exemplary lives, contributed value to society in some special way, attained enlightenment, and so on, to such a profound degree that they now hold sway. These elevated spirits, of high moral character, wisdom and compassion, now have the power to reach across the abyss of death to help the living. *If they so desire.* And why should they so desire? This is the reasoning, in various traditional spiritual systems, for why we propitiate and placate "the dead." We take the time and offer considerable effort to the uttering of their names and the refreshing of their Ka, or spirit, with offerings so they **will** desire to assist us-- we who are still trudging away on the earth plane. This is a timeless spiritual science.

This science, this mystery tradition of spirit placation and ancestral reverence, is important to consider in the context of procreation. When a woman gives her womb over to a man she is, even if unwittingly, supplanting the respective presiding spirit of the place– Not to mention the ancestral spirits of her lineage who are responsible for leading the family to God, to truth, to well being, etc. Women today have sexual encounters and procreate far too often without conferring with the Great Spirit.

What's the moral social indicative of your bloodline? Your district? What's the mission statement of your family? Your tribe? What's the heartfelt world-bettering injunction calling out from the preeminent Spirit holding court where you reside?

Here, in Greenbelt, Eleanor Roosevelt is adamant: "No more secret wars." A clear directive almost at the heart of the country, just some 13 miles outside of Washington D.C. I'm not a politician or activist or anything grandiose like that, but I know enough to imagine the hidden manipulations of the government. And not just in this county. I can't help but ruminate on the alphabet soup of organizations responsible for the secret wars Mother Eleanor Roosevelt is speaking of. And surely many would say it's impossible to end the secret wars– the clandestine plots and manipulations of certain societies, agencies, and groups which allow us to enjoy our Starbucks in peace. Certainly we should be grateful for that peace, perhaps no matter the cost. I know that the untying of such knots can be tedious and messy, but that's the whole point of calling on the Great Spirit.

If we at the very least acknowledge spirit, in this case Mother Elenor Roosevelt, we would be fed tidbits of information-- given epiphanies of a profound nature, such that we could accomplish that seemingly unimaginable and unthinkable task of ceasing secret wars. There **is** a way. Spirit has access to more data than

13

we do. Obviously. Spirit contains all the experiences– failures as well as successes– of all of the people who walked this earth just like us and faced similar challenges. Why should we reinvent the wheel? Why should we paint ourselves into the same corners? Why should we, as a society, make the same mistakes generation after generation when we have access to a world economy of Spirit?

Ritual Meditation: Spirit of Place

Supplies:
White candle
Glass of water
Incense
Fruit
Mugwort

Bathe well using black soap and black salt then splash Florida Water all over your body. Take your supplies with you to a cozy, private place. Smudge the area with sage then light the candle and place the glass or cup of water (glass if home, paper cup if in nature). Light the incense and stick it into the ground, safely away from any kindling. Take the fruit and touch it to your body at the crown of your head, heart, and feet while praying:

"Great spirit of the crossroad, I greet you and ask permission to pass... Great Spirit, Holy Spirit, be with me in this place. I who am known as: _____. Daughter/son/child of _____, daughter/son/child of _____. I bring offerings of fruit, water, light and incense for the Great Spirit.

Greetings to the Holy Spirit of this place. Gratitude to the Holy Spirit of this place. Angels and guides of the Most High hear my petition, grant my prayer. I wish to perceive the spiritual mandate of this place. How may I help fulfill the great plan? How may I fulfill my highest destiny here? Please come forth to guide me. Dua Ruach Hakodesh. Dua Great Spirit. Ase Amen."

Pray from your heart. Speak from your heart. Open your mouth and ask what needs to be asked or say whatever needs to be said. Nature is alive. Spirit is all pervasive. Using our breath, we connect.

After praying/speaking aloud, close your eyes and breathe... Inhaling deeply so that your belly extends, pushing the navel outward. Hold for as long as comfortably possible. Then, exhale... drawing your navel in tight. Hold for as long as comfortably possible. Repeat again and again. Dwell in the in between. Listening. Thoughts quieting. With practice you'll begin to notice thoughts coming into your awareness which are not your own, not originating with you. Don't be afraid. With this ritual we are simply expanding beyond our accustomed boundaries, encompassing the larger non-localized self.

*It will help to keep in mind that this work is about building a relationship. Results will vary and may take time. Someone who has a bloodline connection to the Orishas for example would get a speedier reply from Eleggua/Elegba. He is a crossroad spirit, THE crossroad spirit, responsible for opening and closing the doors which allow our prayers to be heard. Eleggua also opens the doors to opportunity and progress, but only **if** the right choice is made at the proverbial fork in the road.*

Don't hesitate to insert the names of the God or spirit guides of your lineage. Start with what you know.

15

For the next week, watch your dreams and write them down in a journal. Listen for whispers. With time, a spirit guide or angel will come forth to guide you further.

"We need things to be physical."
~Dreamtime

We grow so accustomed to our stationary, physically dense material existence that the idea of spirit contact can frighten us. I recall screaming and jumping up out of bed countless times when I was younger. Once, at boarding school in Philly, I was falling asleep in my cubicle. That's how the dorms were arranged– half walls between designated cubicle spaces. A bed built into the wall, standard green semi-hard mattress, 5 foot wide wardrobe, long desk built into the half wall. At the beginning of senior year I had chosen the cubicle at the very end. Lights out was the sign to go to sleep but I liked to listen to music first. Eyes closed, headphones attached to my oversized black radio/CD player, relaxed to that point between sleep and wakefulness. Feeling a presence I looked up, expecting to see one of my female classmates walking toward me for some last minute conversation about God knows what. Instead I saw a spirit, whitish from head to toe, floating down the narrow hall to my space. And scream. I bolted outta there like a bat outta hell. In hindsight, how I got up the nerve to run past the spirit I don't know. But there was only one way in and one way out– I wasn't sticking around to see what it wanted. For the entirety of the semester I slept down the hall in Kelly's bottom bunk. My cubicle was good for nothing but storage. Thank you Kelly.

Why that fear response though? Maybe the spirit was going to give me good news. For some reason there's this knee jerk instinct to run. I know better now of course, but I was young and that was my first contact with a visible form. I've since told my spirit guides to be kind-- that I prefer NOT to see them. So they usually send me signs and symbols. Works for both of us.

When I told my dad about the experience he said, rather dry long so in his South Philly way, "spirit wasn't gone hurt you." Could've fooled me. I figured if it was coming bearing rainbows and good news then I should have gotten a memo. Can't spirits introduce themselves before popping up unannounced? There must be some sense of common courtesy, I thought to myself. Years later I learned that's a major benefit of regularly working with one's own spiritual court. When we make nice with our guides-- setting regular times for communion-- they don't have to burst onto the scene in a huff after years of neglect and multiple failed attempts to get a message through.

We're born with certain guides who wish to assist us on our journey, for various reasons. Some may have experiences to share which will help with a specific challenge. Others have negative karma to work out and assisting the living clears their tab so to speak. When I was in a quasi-abusive relationship, for example, my Pomba Gira spirit guide revealed her willingness to help via dreamtime. I was at rock bottom. No real money of my own, nothing but my burgeoning rediscovered self-love. She lent me her fierceness, her vivaciousness. On one occasion, she came during dreamtime stark naked and gorgeous. Pure sexuality. Pomba Gira is that backed-into-a-corner divine feminine epiphany-- if my sexuality is all I got, then dammit so be it! That sexuality becomes a means for control of the situation, if nothing else. I found myself mounting my boyfriend more often, straddling, commanding the love making with words that dripped with honey. A firm sweetness. She taught me that I was no man's slave. No worthless pawn in anyone's game. Thank you Pomba Gira! Salve!

I can see the danger here though too— and why from a Abrahamic perspective idols are a major no no. Full stop. The taking down of Asherah poles, the cautionary remarks regarding the witch of Endor and such in the Bible, the full destructive expression of self-love-gone-mad in the case of Jezebel— who as a matter of fact sought the ruin of any prophets who crossed her path. Power is a dangerous drug.

If I had stopped there, feeling myself, I'd be in trouble. But because I dealt with my full spiritual court I was given a wider view and able to look up... beyond just Pomba Gira. See, Santa Clara came to me in the dreamtime too. I was shown a building where people were suffering. Some were being burned by fire, as men held torch machines, blowing and waving the flame back and forth across the terrified crowd. Others were fleeing gunfire but not escaping. There were various scenes of torment... and the sound of people screaming in agony. Off in another room there was a glowing presence floating above a table. I heard/knew "Santa Clara." She had no physical form, no attributes of skin color or any identifiable traits. Just pure peace, holding space. There were devotees beneath her placing candies and other offerings at her feet. She was showing the path to freedom, away from suffering— the path of devotion to God.

Santa Clara, or Saint Clare, was a noble woman who gave everything up to be a nun in the early 1200's A.C. But she didn't just become a nun, she was the first woman to write a formal rule organizing the religious life of women housed communally within the Catholic Church— a rule ultimately ordained by the sitting Pope. The guidelines Saint Clare came up with are still being followed by various sisterhoods across the world to this day– The Rule of Saint Clare.

So on one hand I've got Pomba Gira waving the banner of sexual liberation, and on the other Santa Clara hearkening me to the cloister. Our spiritual court of guides can be funny like that. The dark path and the light path, and never the twain shall meet, right? No. For me they had a head on collision. Within me, and the house I've started, these truths meet headlong and demand integration. This is where context makes all the difference. You could go to a house of Ifa/Lukumi and dance in the light as a child of Obatala till you're blissed out on purity– but you'd be doing yourself and the truth a disservice. Conversely, you could go to a house of Quimbanda/Palo Mayombe and dance in the dark with goetic demons and quasi-deified dead until you're drunk on power and revenge. But still, a disservice.

An example… Once a young lady came to me for divination. She was of European descent, quirky and clearly touched with spiritual gifts. I used Stones & Shells plus Ifa and both confirmed that she was called to be a nun– to live in full devotion to God. She had even dreamed a few nights before of Osa Nla, a name of Obatala which she'd never heard before. However, when I gave her one of the spiritual remedies made clear through Ifa, she balked. I told her she'd need to offer fish to an Orisha. The young lady had a problem with harming animals. The idea of killing one, directly or indirectly, even for a deity, made her squeamish. She protested and I haven't heard from her since. The irony is– if we stop sinning, animal sacrifice wouldn't be necessary. But this is a perfect example of how frilly white we like to get with our spirituality, too pure to be sullied by the darker aspects of this world. Too snobbish to look our own sin and darkness in the face.

Now when I say this half-way-in approach to spirituality is a disservice I mean that enlightenment is in the full encompassing of the mental projection that is our reality. It's an inner and outer truth. In denying killing, murder, and violence one closes off the mind to understanding the nature of reality itself. Because, whether we like it or not, killing and murder exist. Is our God so infantile that He/She/They/It would fail to think of this? Would God somehow create an aspect of experience and not have a way to integrate it into the larger whole for the larger good? Of course not. So in my experience any religious tradition which does not take the darker aspects into consideration, giving actual tools of application, is an anemic tradition. Half of a coin. Look to Ifa, for example. Within this spiritual system the urge to murder and destroy is integrated, just as in the Bible, through animal sacrifice. And only an advanced adherent earns the right to bear the knife. Such an adherent's psyche is willingly anchored to a codified system of mores, values, and deific forms.

This is a fallen world, so of course some portion of humanity would harbor a dark desire to get out, to end it all– for oneself or others, in some way. It's a natural though dangerous-if-unchecked response. But why? Where does this dark inclination come from? What makes our world fallen? It's fallen because of sin. Animal sacrifice requires a person to look at the blood and death which resulted from whatever personal sin was committed. We must look at our fallen-ness. The animal takes the hit to remove any guilty karma from the sinner, dying in his/her/their place. But it was never supposed to be a long term way of life, this animal sacrifice business. Hence the New Testament call to follow Christ. To mitigate sacrifice and animal cruelty, to root out our darkness and penchant for violence, we must start by reversing the first cardinal sin. We must follow Mary. We must follow Aset.

Back to the Pomba Gira/Santa Clara paradox. How can BOTH be true? How did this apparent split– the whore vs. the saint– get resolved for me? Easily… in the self-realization that I am *God's* whore. Everywhere I go His name is in my mouth, His will inside me at my deepest core. I love Him as any good wife loves her husband.

Like turning a blind condescending eye on humanity's penchant for killing, it's preposterous, the idea that God didn't preconceive our lust when this whole creation was created. Why should we ignore it as beyond God's purview? Intelligent design, God, scientific origins– whatever you believe is at the source of this life experience, surely there must have been forethought about every aspect of the human psyche. If you believe in God/source energy as an artist weaving a tapestry very deliberately, this will resonate with you. Of course our sexuality is a part of it.

In looking toward Ancient Kemet we see clear evidence of high spiritual science and sexuality merging. The serpent rests coiled at the base of the spine– arat sekhem, or kundalini of Hindu dharma. If left to operate instinctively it can dwell at the lower chakras concerning itself only with the base desires of physical survival, sexual release, and egoic demonstrations of will. But it is meant to be raised to the crown of the head, to be given wings, as seen on the walls of various Kemetic temples. The whorish impulse is redirected to God, so to speak. This is the key of life. Directing these impulses outward leads to death, but directing them upward leads to immortality.

"Give thyself to God, keep you thyself daily for God;
and let tomorrow be as today." – Ancient Kemetic Proverb[a]

Much of the "how" is learned through our mystery school traditions. There must be a certain readiness and devotional piety in place to fully realize these truths. But anyone can receive Direct Revelation, initiated in temples or not. To invite gnosis– an exalted mystic union– one must simply love God MORE. The heart chakra is a bridge from lower to higher. The serpent's skin of lust is shed through devotional love of God. It is God who shows us directly how He/She/They/It wants to be loved. And the funny thing is, God shares our desire, meets us there in the midst of it. Whatever the nature of our lust, it holds a piece of the puzzle. There's some truth in it that must be pursued and realized. For example, brace yourself– if a woman has a rape fetish, rather than giving herself over to the wild brutality of random men she can give herself to God with the same wild abandon. And believe me, He will come. But it's never malicious. This stems from a desire to feel God's power rushing over one's being in entirety. If we only believe in the physicality of life, we invite real rape, madness, and abuse. But if we believe and KNOW that spirit is just as real, we can experience spirit. Spirit is just as valid as matter, if not moreso.

I was shown this as Father Mother, YabYum. That's the direct revelation I was given – RADA. Before I knew anything about idyllic Vrindaban and Krishna's dalliances, I saw Radha and Krishna making love in a grove, enclosed in a circle of

---

[a] Sebai Muata Ashby, "Egyptian Proverbs" (pg. 59)

ecstatic pairs. Krishna multiplied Himself to be with every woman, every gopi, simultaneously. Father and Mother merged.

The download: Matter, like mater, is mother– the womb of life. She is the ground of experience, the realm of water and earth. While, on the other hand, father is spirit– the realm of thought, visible in fire, unemotional and detached like air. To unite the two is to create an alchemical reaction resulting in epitomized manifestations– Christ, Heru, Krishna, Buddha etc. God is thus brought down to earth. God is in this case the seed bearing Father.

Isis, Mary… we've already been shown the way. Now it's time for us to implement the way on a mass scale. The hunch in our gut to distrust religions is rooted in an innate knowing that we were never meant to just kneel and follow any one idol. Christ Himself said He was "the way the truth and the life." He means to follow Him, not just to worship Him on Sundays. To follow Him, as women, we must trace His life back to the womb He sprang from. That's where He began.

As priestesses we must take position and bring the light down– through our wombs and through our work. Build your inner fire and seek Him. Merge the devotion of Santa Clara with the passion of Pomba Gira…

Ritual
Merging Sinner and Saint, Holifying the Whore

It helps to literally make these things physical. I suggest setting up a meditation space with red roses and a red candle on the left side, then white roses and a white candle on the right side. Imagery would also help. It's easy and free to pull up a couple pictures via Google. Think about the meanings just by looking at them on your phone. Just remember we're not worshiping the images, we're meditating on them— studying them. In this way we invite greater insight about the spirit itself. You'll get a download or epiphany of some sort if your commitment to the work is there.

Simply sit before the candles and meditate on these archetypes, occasionally closing your eyes. What do you see? You may initially stir up feelings of resentment, repression, or rage. That's okay. Just watch. Be a witness to whatever emotions come and let them pass.

This ritual meditation allows us to see what isms and dogmas we carry. You may even be able to trace it to the source— Catholic school, a parent, a middle school friend. We get ideas planted in our heads about sex and holiness from various social sources. But what's the truth? There is no separation. If man is taken out of the equation and these seemingly opposed divine feminine archetypes are left to stand on their own, they can be seen as one and the same.

In your mind's eye see and feel the serpent coiled at the base of your spine. Pomba Gira. See her fiery sultry energy rising, desire calling her higher. Sacral chakra charged with sexual passion. Rising. Each chakra she touches spinning with power, glowing as light. Manipura, above the navel, glowing yellow as she meets it. Feel your self-confidence surging. All three lower chakras swirling. Your root chakra, red in color, as the ground of survival— the impetus for life. Earth and blood and bodies. Desire for experience. Sacral chakra, below the navel, swirling orange. Engorged. Wanting to express, to create, to merge with someone or something. Here Pomba Gira dances wildly, the serpent uncoils and rises. Just above the navel, Manipura, your will to dominate and to control pulls you up out of the madness of sexual excess. Yellow fire. Seeking higher still the serpent reaches to the heart chakra, glowing green. Anahata. The desire to love something or someone beyond oneself peaks again, but expression doesn't go through the sexual organs. This time it rises and comes out through the throat and mouth. Swirling as indigo colored light. A prayer uttered aloud. Whispered or shouted at the top of your lungs. The truest desire. The serpent wants wings. Here, matter remembers that she is the bride of Spirit. Here she prays and begs and cries and sings, calling for the Great Spirit to come down to meet her. Energy rising still. Third eye, glowing light, blue like the sky. Perception no longer obstructed by lower physical limitations and petty cravings. Santa Clara's devotion carried her up beyond the desires of the world to a pure desire for God. God is all she seeks and all she sees, here. The crown of the head begins to tingle as waves of energetic light pour over and onto the crown. Washed. Baptized. Born anew.

This exercise is guided but open enough for you to have your own experience, receive your own revelations. It serves as a means of making the pursuit of God tangibly felt. One may live through multiple lifetimes stuck at one particular chakra, fixated on sex or survial, love or egoic will. With this meditation one can explore and release the concerns of each energy center. It is the chakra system which creates the physical projection that we experience and often cling to. If we have blockages or debris in the sacral chakra for example, we would churn out situations and scenarios and relationships that make those issues experience-able so that we may integrate the knowledge and continue reaching higher up the scale. Pomba Gira's power lies in using the sexual energy which could have once bound her to lower experience to instead propel higher. The realization dawns that her sexual impulse was a liability as long as it kept her dancing with shadows... duality does not exist. All is a projection of mind.

"Henceforth I will go to the gentiles."
Acts 18:6

I was minding my business, pursuing initiation as a sangoma, when YahUah pressed hard on my spirit. After a year or so He called me to serve as His shepherd and prophet. Here I was– chicken-offered, bathed in blood, and calling on ancestors at the top of my lungs– when He showed up in my dreams glowing in the monstrance saying, "Come to Me."
"You want me to be a Catholic?" I thought to myself. "What?? No, that can't be right."

I even went to a Catholic church to visit the Shrine of Our Lady of Częstochowa and attempted to make confession. Looking down at the shiny patent leather shoes of the white priest, Father Tim, I knew in my spirit– "this isn't my father." In a broad humanitarian sense perhaps, but not in a way that fully resonated. I had to go through my lineage– a sangoma reads bones afterall.

So I continued my training process, trying to integrate the download. It was after the sangoma initiating me made a snide comment about Jesus that I had to abandon her as my teacher. He was hanging on the wall of a house she was considering for purchase. A very typical crucifix. "When I walked in the dining room, I just got sad," my sangoma teacher said during our Zoom meeting. We asked her why, as she tried to keep a straight face, all of us staring at our screens while trying to keep our heads bowed. Pointing to the crucifix on the wall in the photo she replied, "I just wanted to take him down and set him free." Everyone laughed.

Jesus is a running joke in many of our African-centered spiritual houses. And understandably so... Slavery. Colonization. Genocide. Religious persecution under whip and threat of death. Many of our ancestors were forced to convert to Abrahamic traditions, or else. So yes, we hold a grudge. What was done in Jesus' name was horrendous. But, He (Yeshua) can and will speak for Himself.

It's the job of the prophet to hear and to keep God's will in play, to make it a part of the social conversation. It's not always convenient or pretty, but Father God's voice can't be ignored. And that's the bit that made it click for me. Father God. Here we were as twazas (initiates) calling on our ancestors, mothers and fathers and great great grandmothers and grandfathers, and back beyond remembering. Father God. As twazas we were calling on "God" but the Jesus face was just unpalatable. There was a disconnect.

My own dreams had shown me He was real. The ancestors even appeared in dreamtime revealing I was called by Isithunywa– that's the prophetic spirit in sangoma culture. An ancestor who "prayed a lot" and "dealt with the Bible" was calling me... to Father God. There is an order to creation. All that "man is the head of the household" stuff was true. And I hated to admit it. I had ended abusive relationships, and was deeply immersed in Goddess spirituality but I saw my ancestral fathers in dreamtime clear as day offering to lead me and I knew in my gut that it's their job to do so.

Men are striving after Amen, the hidden man aka the hidden God. In either case, they are tasked with leading the cows to safe pasture. It's beautiful really. The man on the cross symbolism– man must negate himself for the sake of God's plan and for the

29

sake of any woman he is tasked to lead or support. Everything born of man dies… yet he shepherds and supports even to the point of giving up his life. And here was my sangoma baba castigating the whole concept as laughable. "Forgive them Father for they know not what they do."

You may be wondering why I chose to leave the sangoma training process, if Father God is rooted in ancestors anyway. Couldn't I just stay and endure the snide comments, knowing the truth for myself? No. The ancestors showed me several times that I was to leave, they showed me that this teacher and I would part ways– And it hurt. I had grown to love this woman like family. She was wise, funny, and seriously committed to helping African descendants in America reconnect to our ancestors… To unlock our medicine. But, just reconnecting and venerating ancestors is not enough.

In a dream I was shown a dead twaza– one of the initiates training beside me. She had hung herself with rope by an open door. A horde of young children ran into the room from behind me, from the other direction, and threw quarters at the dead twaza's body. In sangoma tradition, it's common to insist that a person put at least one quarter on the mat to speak to an initiate or sangoma. We channel automatically, so in order to speak to one of us some sort of financial gift is required. It's a matter of respect. In this case, Holy Spirit was making His own snide comment: Unless your spiritual house is engaging in, promoting, and teaching the work of *divine conception*, under the will of Mkhulu– aka the Most High Father, aka Ruach HaKodesh– that work is in vain. Unacceptable. That work then becomes witchcraft devoid of light and life.

I met with my teacher and explained to her all that was going on in my head. The dreams. The Jesus stuff. I explained my need to not only wear white but to be veiled... A makeshift nun's habit. But when I came to a group meeting online wearing all white attire and a veil it was the last straw for her. My baba insinuated that I should leave. This is understandable because it's her house... to a large degree. But, to an even larger degree, it's God's house. He should always get the last word.

One of the first dreams I shared with my sangoma baba prefaced what was to come. I saw myself sitting in a chair in her house as she was speaking to her initiates in another room. I was off to the side. There was a spirit in another room. At the time I presumed it to be a Madama spirit. It looked like a black cloth doll I had made for my own Madama guide– but this wasn't <u>my</u> Madama. Baba was speaking but I knew it was the female spirit speaking through her. Referring to me, Baba said to the twazas: "She's enlightened– a prophet."

I didn't tell Baba about this dream for several months because it felt like tooting my own horn. As far as I was concerned, I'm nobody– just a spiritual seeker trying to figure this life out like everybody else; trying to learn how to deal with my ancestors. Why should I be quick to tell Baba that the ancestors called me an enlightened prophet? Wouldn't the spirits show her directly? Maybe. But, as I eventually comprehended, a huge part of the twaza process entails sharing dreams with one's teacher, one's Baba or Gogo. That's how the initiation teachers determine what our ancestors want. Regrettably, when I finally did share the "She's a prophet" dream with my teacher, it was dismissed. Nothing about my initiation process changed... Not even when Isithunywa itself came to claim me.

31

But even from just this Madama dream it was clear– my process must be different. Despite my attempts to follow house protocols, I was not like the other twazas. I would yoy til I was hoarse and hot in the face trying to call my ancestors but all that usually came out was, "I si si si si si si si ... I si sisisis." Also dismissed.

In another instance, after shouting to my ancestors while Baba was shouting at me, I found myself drawing my name on the floor– as the spirit who came refused to speak. It felt like my body was immovable– just an unfathomable silence and erect-spine stillness. When Baba asked the spirit its name, He used my index finger to trace out the letters S-H-I-V-J-I on Baba's hardwood floor.

Baba didn't know it, and neither did I really, but these were Mami Wata spirits. Or maybe she did have an idea. Who knows. Either way, it's been said that these spirits don't fully respond to priests outside their lineage. So what was I doing there? I asked myself that question every day after the first unfruitful year of twazahood.

One day while going about my normal twaza routine at home I heard a voice whisper: "Khulu Clan." In South Africa grandmothers are called "Gogo" while grandfathers are called "Mkhulu." Nkulunkulu is the supreme Father deity known to inhabit mountains. The highest of the heights. The Grandfathers were reassuring me that I had a right and a reason to be there.

So I continued to follow initiation protocols, but it still felt off somehow. "Trust the process," my sangoma baba always reminded us. So I did. And she was right. The confusion eventually gave way to lucid assurance. I had a distinct message that was coming from the ones who sent me: Teach and honor

32

Father God's will regarding *divine conception* or there will be death... Inevitably. Not necessarily as a punishment from God but as a natural result of neglecting *divine conception*. Not only did I dream that a twaza died, but sometime later I saw my sangoma baba in the hospital, infected with the Corona Virus. This hospital warning was summarily rejected as impossible just before my departure from her spiritual house.

One evening while I was still in the thick of it, we were all together online as a group, all the twazas kneeling and listening attentively via Zoom. Baba showed us a YouTube video of sangomas in South Africa up in the mountains. I saw the Madama spirit from my "she's a prophet" dream clear as day—felt it in my bones on sight. It turned out that the Madama spirit who channeled that message in my dream was actually the woman who had trained my sangoma baba many years ago. Her own deceased initiator was saying that my process had to be different. And, in the dream, she was saying it through the mouth of my sangoma baba herself! If a sangoma teacher doesn't respect THAT, what else would a sangoma teacher respect???

The twaza who hung herself in my other dream had already endured 3 years of training by the time I showed up. The process would go on "until the ancestors show graduation signs in dreams," we were told. I wanted wholeheartedly to graduate according to plan and serve the community as a sangoma. But, eventually I conceded that what I want is always second to God's want. The ancestors and Holy Spirit showed me in dreams that my time with Sangoma Baba was done. It had been almost a year and a half. After being verbally double-teamed by Sangoma Baba and one of her long-graduated daughters for over two hours, while kneeling, I finally conceded.

> *"But when they opposed themselves and became abusive, Paul shook out his clothes in protest and said to them, "Your blood be on your own heads! I am innocent of it. Henceforth I will go to the Gentiles." Acts 18:6*

Since leaving that spiritual house the messages have only gotten louder. I learned to study the Bible instead of waiting on my sangoma teacher to explain things. It was as if the words swirled around on the page and stood out in bold letters with messages just for me. I found Asar/Osiris in those pages. I found truth buried beneath generations of lies.

Eyeh Asher Eyeh for example. We've been told that this means "I Am That I Am." Lies. When Moses received the Ten Commandments from God he asked, "who shall I say has sent me?" According to Exodus 3:14, "Eyeh Asher Eyeh" was God's reply. If we look at the original Hebrew letters we are led to ASR. Iah was a "moon God" in ancient Kemet. Ah also means "great." ASR is the God "Asar" (aka Osiris), as the names were written without vowels in the original Hebrew and Kemetic languages. Iah = Yah. So the Lord's reply was: Iah Asr Iah. Yah Asar Yah. Moon God Asar, Moon God or The Great Asar Great Moon God. Many depictions of Mother Mary show her standing atop a crescent moon.

I already knew that Asar/Osiris was the hidden or dead God often depicted standing or sitting enthroned near Isis/Aset. But to learn that Asar was the God of the Bible... That's when I dropped the book and ran.

If I had obeyed Sangoma Baba and followed her house protocols to the letter I never would have made this discovery. Twazas don't read. They don't watch TV. Twazas mostly just sit on a mat on the floor and commune with their ancestors, after rigorous praying. Well thank God my ancestral communing led me to pick up the Bible and compare it with the Prt m Heru and other holy texts. Father God was giving me breadcrumbs to follow. That's how the Holy Spirit operates. He moves us with whispers and gentle nudges. Eventually, after running from it, I picked the Bible back up. There was much more to learn.

Let me stop to mention here that while still with the sangoma, my Isithunywa & Inglozi spirits took over the initiation process. They prompted me to fast, wear white, read the Bible, and pray. It was all about deepening my prophetic gift and clarifying God's plan for my life.

For 45 days I fasted, taking only coconut milk and water. This wasn't allowed for twazas because we're supposed to feed our ancestors. So, in secret I fasted– all the while singing, dancing and doing twaza tasks. The downloads kept coming. In this way, Holy Spirit brought clarity to my Christ vs. ancestors confusion. Come to find out, they're not mutually exclusive.

The next major fast was on water alone. My plan was 40 days. Afterall, the coconut milk fast wasn't as hard as I expected. But by day 3 on only water I had second thoughts. My mind seemed foggy, my body heavy. By day 6 I felt like I was going to die. So I prayed. And Spirit responded: Aim for 8.

I'd love to tell you I was the picture of piousness, kneeling in prayer at my shrine with a serene expression. No. I took to the bed. Found myself moaning and begging Father God for an

Impossible Burger. Even discovered a whole new sector of YouTube: Mukbangs. Something about fasting always made me feel disconnected from everyone and everything around me. Luckily there was no one here to see me look like death warmed over. I admit that it did feel a bit like cheating, but those mukbangs were a source of much needed comfort. Helped me remember that one day soon the fast would end. I would enjoy this life like everyone else again.

With an end goal in sight, 8 days, I was able to settle into the shedding. It felt like years of sin were falling off my body and out of remembering. I knew I was being forgiven. Khulu Clan saw the lengths I was willing to go to in order to find, serve, and please God. Both my Fathers and my Mothers were pleased. Eventually, sometime around day 7, I noticed bulimia and anorexia videos kept popping up on my feed. YouTube's algorithm countering the mukbangs? Maybe. But, paired with dreams, after day 8 I perceived confirmation that my water fast was over. Even though I was instructed to aim for 8 days, still I wanted that additional confirmation that it was okay to stop. That's my nature as a gopi, as a devotee, as a wife of God. If those confirmations didn't come... somebody would have found me eventually. That was my thinking. "Thy will, not my will, be done."

Warning: I do not advocate this type of fast for ANYONE. Consult a doctor, a priest, or whatever is necessary for you. This is just how I do things. It gets me results. The mad gibberish uttered during and after my fastings is what's written in these pages. Painfully wrought epiphanies.

"Do you love me? Feed my sheep."
John 21:15-25

This next revelation caused me to just sit and stare into space, again... After His crucifixion and resurrection, after dealing with the doubting of Thomas, in John 21:15-23 Yeshua/Jesus speaks with one of His disciples candidly:

> *When they had finished eating, Jesus said to Simon Peter, "Simon son of John, do you love me more than these?"*
> *"Yes, Lord," he said, "you know that I love you."*
> *Jesus said, "Feed my lambs."*
> *Again Jesus said, "Simon son of John, do you love me?"*
> *He answered, "Yes, Lord, you know that I love you."*
> *Jesus said, "Take care of my sheep." The third time he said to him, "Simon son of John, do you love me?"*
> *Peter was hurt because Jesus asked him the third time, "Do you love me?" He said, "Lord, you know all things; you know that I love you." Jesus said, "Feed my sheep. Very truly I tell you, when you were younger you dressed yourself and went where you wanted; but when you are old you will stretch out your hands, and someone else will dress you and lead you where you do not want to go... Follow me!"*
> *Peter turned and saw that the disciple whom Jesus loved was following them. (This was the one who had leaned back against Jesus at the supper...) When Peter saw him he asked, "Lord, what about him?"*

Jesus answered, "If I want him to remain alive until I return, what is that to you? You must follow me."

A large part of shamanic work is reading between the lines, seeing the forest beyond one tree. Just like when the message came through loud and clear, "Eleanor Roosevelt spirit," immediately upon reading this biblical page, Holy Spirit emphasized certain portions of the text. It was as if the words swirled on the page and made themselves bold. I just knew— this was a dialogue between lovers. Like any modern romantic interlude we might witness today, one partner playfully asks the other, "Do you love me? Do you really love me?" That playfully-asking partner might go on to request some sweet notion, some demonstration of said love... "If you love me you'll take me to the movies tomorrow night." Or, "if you love me you'll smile at Thanksgiving dinner while you tolerate my family." It's like playfully telling one's partner, "Brace yourself, I'm going to ask something of you. If you love me, it will be easy to carry out."

This could also be a relationship of another sort, as between family members. But if it was, in this case, I doubt Yeshua would have pushed that love button three full times. Even Simon Peter was "hurt" by being asked so many times. It was as if Yeshua was doubting his love.

So, to prove his devotion, Simon Peter confirmed that he loved his Lord, Yeshua, and gave no refusal to follow Him and feed His sheep. The only qualm appeared when Simon Peter looked back and saw Yeshua's other lover, who remains unnamed. Less playfully, Yeshua rebuttals, "What is it to you?" Is this perhaps Yeshua's advocacy of free love? Polygamy? Not necessarily. Yeshua doesn't try to mush the two men into a joint tryst, quite the opposite. He basically tells Simon Peter to relax and focus on the love he has for him alone... i.e. don't get distracted by petty jealousies. The other lover is not to be harmed. Don't hurt a hair on his head.

So if we follow this line of thinking further, what we're seeing here is a calling to not only feed and take care of Yeshua's sheep in general, but the context here is: feed and take care of *those who love the way Yeshua loved*. The rainbow people– LGBTQ+. *Dropped the book again right about there.*

Yeshua warns Simon Peter that he's being called into adulthood now. He advises him, saying that when he was young he got to go and do as he pleased. But this calling would take Simon Peter into unfamiliar, and likely undesired, territory. I think of how many staunch Christians, Catholics and the like may read this and fight it tooth and nail– not wanting to go there, even if God Himself issued the rainbow-colored proclamation.

Personally, I didn't choose this road either. I was enlisted. YahUah sent a storm. I danced and sang, twaza style, while watching the rain outside my screen door. Then, a rainbow appeared. But it wasn't up high in the sky, rather it was low, arching over a tree just near my second floor patio. I can be heard on camera exclaiming, "It's in my yard y'all! Not up in the sky... it's right here!" I wasn't "out" yet, wasn't even thinking about sexuality actually– just trying to get through my sangoma initiation. But the calling was loud and the biblical pointings were mounting, in support of the callings.

To me, it's kinda like a logic puzzle, "if then" statements: If Iah Asar Iah is the true God of the Bible, if Isis/Aset was devoted to Asar and produced a divine child without physical intercouse, then it makes sense that Iah-Shua/Yah-Shu-Aah would promote homosexual relationships as a means of avoiding a repeat of that great and shameful fall in Eden. The one where Eve offered the fruit to Adam, egged on by a wiley snake up an "I know better than God" tree.

I've always loved logic puzzles but I admit, this one made me a little dizzy. Also a little perturbed. Why wasn't I taught this? Why was I forced to match up with Eric Last-Name-Forgotten in elementary school for an impromptu class dance before I even knew what my sexual nature really was? Insert reverse groomer pun here.

I also admit that, like it probably hit for Simon Peter, this "go forth and champion gay rights" thing took me aback. Here I am pursuing ancestors, seeking God– priestess of holy stuff– and then here's Yah leading me into the gay arena. Didn't see that coming.

Regardless, if there was some latent untapped holiness to homosexuality, I prayed to be shown. Again I was reminded of that dream of Radha and Krishna– when Spirit revealed the word RADA surrounded by male and female figures in various sexual positions. It was Krishna multiplying Himself to be with each woman. "I am the seed giving Father." (Bhagavad Gita 14.4)

We must let God be God. Yeshua showed men the way to walk in humility, in deference. They're being called to take up their crosses and swallow this uncomfortable, sometimes inconvenient truth in order to help resuscitate our dying world. We have literally walked into the valley of the shadow of death. Time for us to turn around and go the other way.

John 10:11-18 - The Good Shepherd lays down his life…

So, if everything born of man dies and Yeshua is shepherding gay/lesbian/queer sheep... now what? We stop having so much sex. That's how I heard it. This is the natural conclusion of the logic puzzle. **If:** everything born of man dies + Yeshua was actually King of the Queers,* **then**: We must stop having so much sex. <u>We've been doing it wrong!</u> To determine how to do it right we must first turn to our clearest example of doing it wrong: Eve. Genesis is fitting food for any student of world religion– for any mystic seeking personal gnosis..

They say that Eve is the mother of all the living. They say that this is the meaning of her name, Chava, in the original Hebrew. But, it is Chaya which denotes life. Whereas chai denotes life, lichyot denotes to live, and chayah denotes living one. The v or vav in Chava connects this mother of the fall to the serpent: Chivya. If Eve was the mother of all the living she would have been named Chaya.

It is key that Eve is called Chava and not Chaya. Chaya contains a y, a Yod, the letter signifying God's hand. Chava's v, or vav, signifies a hook or nail-- she fell for the serpent's lies, hook line and sinker. In Kemetic terms, Eve/Chava did not take hold of the serpent and turn it around. The goal is to raise the serpent to the crown of the head. Instead, Eve succumbed to lust devoid of God's will.

---

*Note: Queer is not necessarily synonymous with sodomy here.

To break it down even further:

Chava = Chet+Vav+Heh.
Separation wall + hook/nail/peg + behold.
The Ch or chet is symbolized by a fence/tent wall, alluding to separation or enclosure. The v or vav is symbolized by a nail/peg/hook alluding to binding. The heh is behold.

Whereas **Chaya = Chet Yod Heh.**
Separation wall + God's hand + behold.

Separated-- set apart-- in both cases, but for whom?

A nail binds and a hook catches, whereas God's hand holds or uplifts. He exalts. God's hand produces spiritual alignment and peace in the garden– true freedom, whereas Chava/Eve invites suffering by being bound to the serpent and tempting man. All was "good" until Eve shared God's fruit with Adam. And this, for a nun especially, is the cardinal sin... sharing the fruit with man. It is akin to dabbing a toe into a mirage, into the illusionary waters of apparent duality. It was as if woman reached out into the darkness and made love with a shadow. A figment. An illusion. In reality there are not two. There is only one. This is the meaning behind the famous Biblical/Torah prayer known as Shema Israel:

Shema Yisra'el, Adonai Eloheinu, Adonai Echad.
Hear Israel, YHWH is our God, YHWH is One.

God is one. Non-dual.

It's the one thing we are never to forget, driven home again and again in various verses: Deuteronomy 6:4-9, 11:13-22, Numbers 15:37-41, Mark 12:30-31. Love God. This is the root behind the command to love thy neighbor. Love, not lust. Ahava, not eros. God is the true receptacle of all our loves– whether as Father, Brother, Lover, or Friend. With visualized form or as formlessness, we are to love Him. The choice is ours.

God is one. No second is needed for procreation because all are one. Advaita vedanta is the heart of biblical truth and a core reality of our world.

The Bible is a layered text bearing the timeless truth of non-duality.

Now back to the "set apart for who?" question. A woman is either for God or she is for man. Depends on her calling. In Kemetic terms, God is Amun/Amen– the hidden man. Min is a deity with an erect phallus and a whip. Men can be seen on pyramid walls propitiating this deity. They are the visible expression of the deity Min. But, as nuns and daughters of Aset, our job is to seek the hidden man– Amen/Amun.

It's a beautiful and maddening dance, this earth thing. To be so obviously and often frustratingly condensed into such density, into physical matter. Women have the power to either bind us deeper into matter or to free us of physical limitation. To wed God brings such freedom.

For generations it's seemed so obscure. As if women with a calling to serve as priestesses or as nuns are just romantic fools, chasing after some never-attainable Father fairy in the sky. But Father God is very real and knowable. I've seen the trees burning with the fire of Yah's Yod. I've heard Him whisper "Come to Me."

Our task is to wed spirit to matter. No longer can we consign this world to the fire of dualistic suffering, perpetuating the falsehood of separation. A priestess must, even in the trenches of physicality, remember and manifest the force and truth of spirit. Ruach burns with a desire to be known.

We've been living out the ultimate truth– growing into acceptance of it. Duality vs non-duality. Masculine and feminine apart vs masculine and feminine unified. We've lived out the union of man + woman, producing offspring through the union of earthly opposites. Now we're poised to finally accept that **Spirit is the true opposite of matter.** Physical + physical = perishability. We've seen the physical manifestation, the interplay of masculine and feminine, for generations. So, you'd think it would now be easy to accept this exalted mystic union **within one being**...

Neither Isis or Mary had any physical male counterpart to assist them in conception. The religious among us are apt to gather around on Sundays, but can we live it? We are called now, beyond the boundaries of religiosity, to see and to serve this ultimate truth of non-duality.

This is our key to a planet-wide renaissance.
KaRaIst is our key to a planet-wide renaissance.

The spirit of Father God, aka Amun-Ra, in mystic union with Isis/Aset, His throne... this is the core operating system of our world.

There is neither Jew nor Greek, there is neither slave nor free man, there is neither male nor female; for you are all one in Christ Jesus.
Galatians 3:28

This is a dangerous book to read. These are dangerous truths to know. For this reason, they have been kept secret for generations, granted directly from teacher to worthy disciple. Both, truth and disciple, are rare jewels. Carrying such truth is akin to carrying fire. You cannot help but to burn. While standing in the checkout line at the local market I have felt it. Or, while sitting on a park bench overlooking the water, watching people go about their business. People-watching can take on an ominous bias– everything tinged by the stain of adharma.

45

Sometimes I feel like the stereotypical prudish nun– seeing everywhere nothing but sin.

When you know the truth you can't unknow it. It seeps into every hidden crevice within the mind. All your longings, your goals, your peace become tethered like an anchor to the true dharma making it excruciatingly painful to move in any other direction. One cannot move away from it. The only option is to follow the pull, to allow the fire to engulf you completely. This is a fire familiar to dakinis, mambos who court Petro lwa, and any natural born priestess consumed with a desire to know God.

Perhaps I should have warned you before you read the first section… because now it is too late. The transmission is of fire and water both. And what will you do with it? Mantra has been given, RADA, and now yantra must unfold. Mantra is a seed that must be played with, watered with constant repetition, until it sprouts– until it reveals direct truth all of its own accord. It's a living thing, God's word. The seed of all creation. It will grow sprouts in you, stretch its roots down into the ground beneath your feet or call you to seek new ground. It's a contagious transmission so if you find yourself in dry hopeless soil you MUST move... Must surround yourself with fertile ears– capable doers. Otherwise what good is it? It's true that a lighthouse must stand alone to some extent, but such a beam also attracts lost ships. Who are you attracting? What will you feed them when they come? Divine conception through mystic union is the lifeblood of our work. To not impart it is to die in the arid soil we cling to. But through teaching this timeless dharma one becomes a fountain of life.

Sisterhood is our yantra. Through sisterhood we are able, each of us, to explore mantra fully without distraction or

46

obstruction. We are burning to know it. This samsaric life could never hold us, we are born with a counter-calling which demands we transcend mundane pursuits. We are born with the gift of recognition– and this is a mercy bequeathed by God. Not everyone will recognize such truth when it's revealed– but you do. So now what? Find the others.

When I was a little girl my dad brought a cartoon movie home for me on vhs tape. This was after my parents had separated. He had the habit of fishing for gifts in those stuffed animal booths– the ones with the big remote control claw. He brought home so many stuffed animals and toys and films for me that my mother had to build a hammock over my bed to hold them all. The Last Unicorn was my favorite acquisition.

The animated story told of King Haggard, an old rusty monarch with a penchant for collecting oddities and holding onto whatever made him happy– a wizard, a juggler, a blessing of unicorns. From his dilapidated castle he could sit and watch his unicorns, imagine them really, beneath the waves of the sea where he had trapped them. Years prior he had sent a red bull out to collect them from the forests. With fiery aggressive corralling the bull led them all to the sea for King Haggard– all except one. Spoiler alert: That one last unicorn penetrated Haggard's dilapidated castle, snuck through the secret passageway (a clock that had to strike the right time), riddled her way past a dead king with a crown of thorns who demanded wine for passage– all of that and ultimately this brave unicorn set her sisters free.

She did this with the help of her own wizard, a vintage damsel who still believed in unicorns, and a brave knight who loved her enough to eventually let her go. This last unicorn had to take on the appearance of a human woman in order to get past the bull and into Haggard's castle. To do this, the young wizard waved his wand calling out, "Magic, do as you will!" I can appreciate that now, the "letting go and letting God" so to speak. God (aka the magic) turned the unicorn into a woman who the magician named Lady Amalthea. But, as even the old King noticed, Lady Amalthea was no ordinary woman. Her hair was white, and her eyes were perplexing. The king complained that he could not see himself in her eyes. Eventually the unicorn inside Amalthea began to forget who she was or why she had even come to this place. Reminds me of Sophia or Shakti getting lost in the Maya. "I can feel this body dying all around me," the unicorn woman cried. But, her friends didn't let her forget. Do you have friends like that? Maybe you're that friend to the sisters waiting on you for their own reminder: Don't fall asleep. Don't get too comfortable in your dilapidated castle.

Fast forward to the end and we see a breathtakingly beautiful scene— a horde of unicorns running atop the waves, out of Haggard's underwater prison and back into the world. We learned in the beginning of the film that unicorns keep their forests alive by their very presence. In Ifa, we learn that women are the mothers of the forest. Dua Iyami.

Without women who know and wield these mysteries, our forests and our world as a whole can only die. Everything born of man dies. Try though they might, the men of this world build up edifices— stone masons, architects, scientists, politicians, and what have you— but always they crumble. Nature itself is our home and there must be greater balance. We will be saved by women who whisper to the trees and flowers, and the men who uphold them— men who entertain such whispers too.

"I accept no intermediary between myself and God."

They say His name is ineffable. That it cannot and should not be pronounced. So we are to say "Lord," or "The God," or YHWH and so on. Anything but the actual name of God. Why? Because to say and to fully comprehend the name of God grants access to becoming that, to merging with that, and then... who would need a priest?

I learned a long time ago that any priest, guru, or teacher who doesn't lead one back to oneself cannot be trusted. In my household, as a kid, I'd hear my parents talking about grown folks' stuff over coffee. My mother had moved us away from my father and into my grandmother's apartment when I was about 7 years old. Grandmom had been sick. But I always looked forward to my dad's visits– whenever Doris (his next common law wife) would let him borrow the car. I'd hear them critique "the powers that be" and try to make sense of their no-punches-pulled social commentaries. One remark always stuck with me, "Religion is the opiate of the people."

That probably had something to do with my parents deciding to let me figure it all out for myself. I remember my mom telling me this very proudly; she didn't want my perception clouded by other people's opinions. She said she felt lied to. "Sometimes I think somebody dropped me off on the wrong planet," she'd lament. Church always seemed to hold something back, to hear her tell it. Rosetta, my mother, eventually up and left America in the 60's for Cuba, Paris and Ghana. She never quite got all the answers though, just men, stillbirths and loneliness. So, in

49

hindsight, I can understand why she'd want me to find the answers for myself. Because she hadn't. But I can tell you it hurt like hell, bumping into all the sharp edges and unpainting myself out of tight corners. Figuring it out has a definite cost. A toll.

Kneeling in front of my now former sangoma baba as she and a senior priestess railed on me was such a moment of sharpness. I paid the "figure it out for yourself" fee for sure. Body aching, mind throbbing sharpness, wondering how I got there. Why was finding the truth so hard? I'm not an idiot (self talk), of course initiation into a spiritual house requires pruning– the breaking of ego... But this is ridiculous! And I realize the initiation process is about putting people through their paces, part pacing and part payback. If the initiator had to walk 10 miles barefoot and sleep in a cave filled with chupacabras (who bit their sleeping guests in the night), then certainly any student who comes knocking will get chupacabras thrown at them. It **can't** be easy. That's just how it goes, right? No!

Maybe it's the Petro/Makaya spirits in me, or the Philly indignation, but we ain't got time for all that. Why would I want my students to endure all the sharp edges I bumped up against? It's my job to make it plain, to spare my daughters from the madness of dating the wrong men, suffering stillbirths and enduring loneliness; to spare them the 10-mile calluses and chupacabras. Life is hard enough. So pacing, yes. Payback, no. Not here. We're up against a sinister intention to withhold information so we don't have time to waste. The name of God must be made effable:

IahUah. YahUah. AahUa. In ancient Kemetic this means Great Oneness. Great One. Allah Akbar– The God is the Greatest.

YHWH, YahUah. There was no "w." Writing in stone required putting a v instead of the curve of the u. So for the oo sound, two v's we're placed. Therefore, the WH of YahWeh is actually Uah. YahUah. IahUah. AahUah. Ua means one/oneness.

Once, in dreamtime, I saw a group of Jewish people in a mall. They were in their own little store area, wearing fancy religious vestments. In the dream I asked aloud, "How can anyone else <u>get it</u> if we can't get in?" It was a restricted club. No access.

We've got to decide, as one humanity residing on this innately beautiful rock— are we ready to be one with God or not? Are we tired of the suffering, the famine, the disease, the death? What have we got to lose? #all-in

Crossing the Polytheistic Bridge

Across cultures and across centuries, the little silver ball has swung back and forth between monotheism and polytheism. Factions from each side arguing in circles. "Which God is supreme?" they debate. The polytheism isn't just over there with the "idolaters" and spiritualists. We've made idols of the religions themselves. Uneditable. Static. Stagnant. Closed systems which each bear "the only truth." From what I'm being shown, our salvation comes from precisely the opposite approach. These religions must be put together, shaken up, stirred, compared. Then we'll see how they complement each other and say the same thing– or at least ultimately point to the same truth of Oneness.

Perhaps to my mother's chagrin, these epiphanies didn't just come to me from reading religious texts. We can't heap up *all* the blame on the various churches. There's a mystic impartation involved. When a devotee desires to know God with enough tenacity, God reaches out to that thirsty soul.

I can remember waking up in the middle of the night or in the morning just knowing something. "There is no separation." "I no longer see duality." Unfamiliar mantras would resound in my mind. From that place of knowing, one can more easily engage in the study of comparative religion because, then, it's not just some sterile abstract study, rather it's a devotional act. So what I'm saying is, for all the Rosettas out there, curious but convinced the religious gatekeepers are holding back or outright lying: Seek for yourself. "Knock and the door will be opened," Yeshua said. So true.

"The seed needs the water, 'fore it grows out of the ground. But it just keeps on getting hard, and hunger more profound."
Make it Rain sung by Ed Sheeran, from SOA
{Played after a dream visitation by Akhenaten, during a rainstorm}

We must cry out to YahUah like thirsty seeds. "Make it rain, make it rain down, Lord..." Then we can each receive direct revelation. Then we can each see for ourselves. While waiting for direct revelation we must give an ear to the prophets. Then, go back to the prayer closet for confirmation on anything said by any such prophets. The truth will speak for itself.

My very gifted wife had a dream recently: She saw the Orishas in a closet. There was a bit of chaos until Orunmila appeared in the closet too. Orunmila is the prophetic spirit within the spiritual system of Ifa. In South Africa it's known as Isithunywa... *the messenger*. Without the prophetic at the heart of our spiritual houses, we're perpetuating chaos and confusion. Partial truths. Throwing parties for Oshun or Yemaya, Ogun or Shango etc. Bembes and rogacions. Without Orunmila there's no one to point to Odudua, and no one to point to Olodumare– the Owner of Everything.

What we have here now is like a polytheistic monotheism. Our Orishas, Amakhosi, Neteru, Devis/Devas, and Buddhas have all been pointing us toward realization of Oneness, divine conception and immortality. It is the prophet who brings it all together. It's the seers, the mystics, the God-chosen edifiers who must come forth to co-sign on these truths. The rain will fall. Lightning will strike. There will be signs.

Our polytheistic monotheism works in stages. The Orishas and various archetypes represent not only an aspect of nature, but **one's very own nature,** at any given point in time. The trap we fall into is thinking "this is my nature for the rest of my life." As though being Oshun-ish at 25 years old means you'll still be Oshun-ish at 65. And maybe you will be, that depends on your calling. But, ideally one moves through the Orisha/Neteru framework as one matures, as one studies and engages in the devotional practices of the deity. My Oshun was with me till darn near 40. But I matured into Oya then Yemaya. And always Obatala was there as my touchstone, bearing wisdom to not get stuck in any one nature. My Ori is a good Ori.

We must resist the tendency to be dogmatic about everything. The above point could easily become a mandate, with initiates being forced by their teachers to change Orishas before the necessary lessons have been learned. AahUah and the ancestors confirm when a different Orisha is in play. But overall, our initiation processes should be fluid, allowing for true spiritual/mental/emotional maturation.

Ultimately, and ideally, one realizes the monotheistic side of the coin– merging with the Great Oneness. The deific personifications, or spiritual archetypes, give way to the formless absolute. It's an everything everywhere simultaneous beingness. THE all pervasive consciousness behind and above and within all forms. The cause and the outcome. The source and goal of all spiritual aspiration. "Be what you are" is the most direct route, but we find ourselves expressing habits, moving through generational curses, and refining our personalities… a process which too often takes decades or even lifetimes. But without a doubt this is a polytheisric bridge, and cross it we must.

We can't merge with the all pervasive ocean if we cling to the side of the pool. It has all been training for something much much greater. After all, God is a function. To realize God one must realize one's function. This is the genius of Ifa, the gift of Orunmila PBUH. This is the gift of God's prophets.

The divination work, with Stones and Shells or what have you, is just practice… preparation for when you plunge into the sea of Oneness. The forces of nature, divination systems, and murtis are tools which can be used so that you are ultimately able to distinguish, draw parallels and interpret three dimensional signs. The Great Oneness gives constant feedback. You yourself are part of this Oneness. Don't be afraid. No more need to cling to the shore, let go and drift in this sea of God's provision, of God's wisdom, of God's all pervasive grace.

Studying the Orishas, Neteru, yidams, murtis and so on has given us comprehension of the multifaceted face of God. Like colors through a prism, they all come from Him. So many have been lost for being unwilling or unable to accept monotheism in the face of a perceived condemnation of cherished idols. The warnings were given so bluntly in various religious texts for edification, for clarity… as a parent lays out clearly right from wrong to spare a child from harm. "Don't touch the hot stove or you'll get burned." "Don't dwell in duality or you'll face the hellfire of your own mental projections and denied integrations." "You'll lose sight of the Supreme, the harmonious big picture, if you focus on only one small pixel." Quran. Bible. Torah. Ifa. No matter how it was said, unfortunately, even those direct religious warnings are often seen as overbearing impositions from God Himself. What kind of a God condemns His people to hellfire anyway? No, better question: What kind of people deny the truth of His all pervasive existence as Oneness... and their own part of that all-pervasive being?

God, Source, YahUah has always been calling us unto Himself, Itself... into this Oneness. So the divination tools (Stones and Shells, Ifa. I-Ching, and such) are a means of comprehending the facets of God and their interplay. But always they lead to the Oneness, to the Owner of Everything...

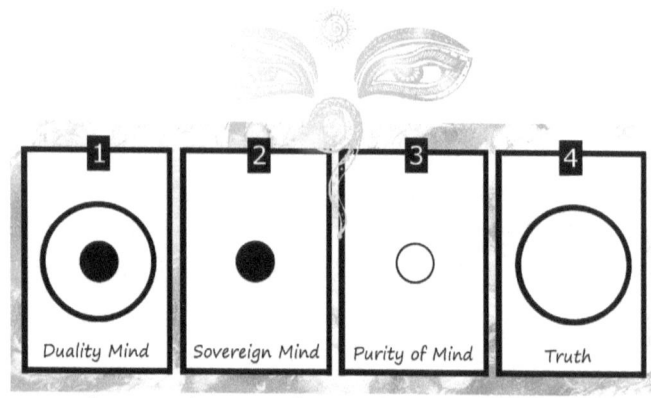

The 4 Phases of Mind in Meditation

1	2	3	4
Awake	Dream	Deep Sleep	Turiya
Creation	Ideal envisioned	Nothingness	Behind the three states
Duality			Non-Duality

A	U	M	—
Create/Not that	Protect/Preserve	Destroy/Dissolve	Blank Slate, Ecstasy

Brahma	Vishnu	Shiva	AahUah/Brahman
Obatala	Warriors/Yemaya	Olokun/Orun/Ogun	Olodumare*
Damballah	Agwe	Baron/Yamakaya	Dharmakaya
			Nameless Absolute
			False dual reality overwritten

Father....................................Dharmakaya
Son..Sambhogakaya
Holy Ghost upon Throne............Nirmanakaya

*The Nameless Absolute/Olodumare is served by Orunmila and Oduduwa, the living mouthpiece and establisher of the Throne of God on earth, respectively.

Only when you
1) have realized that you are "not that" physical
experience/reality,
2) decide what to keep/preserve and
3) destroy everything else
will you perceive the fourth state known as Turiya–
All encompassing Oneness...

Merging with the reality because there's no longer any obscuration or anything other than Self to get hung up on. No likes, dislikes, preferences, desires, fears, traumas, or personality hindrances, no enemies or shadows. All is perceived as Self emanation.

Mother and Child (Isis Heru/Mary Jesus etc) are a vehicle to destroy all that is not God, all that is not truth, all that is not worth preserving.
Holy Spirit hovers over the waters ("M") aka Mem. Feminine receptivity. Womb waters. Mental stillness. This world is thus a co-creation of Father/Mother, YabYum.

Nirmanakaya is the feminine throne of the all pervasive Dharmakaya. Through this interaction, this meeting, the Son— Sambhogakaya/Bliss body— is produced.
The female fully realized buddha is a gateway (a door) to the all pervasive eternal absolute. Sat Chit Ananda. Existence Knowledge Bliss. Absolute Beingness.
The trick is to realize the destruction/abandonment of form latent in the deep dreamless sleep state WHILE STILL AWAKE (not waiting until sleep or death to escape but to do so willingly

and consciously) so that the Holy Spirit can then hover over the waters of your object-less awareness and OVERWRITE the creation according to the original divine blueprint... Replacing falsehood with truth and bliss.

When your realization takes you beyond the localized self to the self in all, this is Turiyata– the state beyond the fourth.

The Mother and Child as divine throne catapults ALL sentient beings into the bliss of the fourth, beyond individual obscurations, to experience the pure truth. Sat Chit Ananda. May the stainless sambhogakaya bliss body pervade all.

The Way is Through Love

"How nice it would be to finally have value— to feel like something more than a castaway." These thoughts come to me frequently, empathically. I see women suffering myriad abuses in my dreams at night— literally tortured by boyfriends or strangers who view them as trash cans, and others raped or stolen away. This book is not just for the priestesses but for the "whores" and "prostitutes" and abuse victims who feel like living breathing refuse. For those who've inherited nothing but concrete and loneliness. The sidewalk is all you have, unless they start charging to walk on it. Trapped in city circumstances, locked in bill schedules, nothing of worth to your name except what's between your legs. Wouldn't it be nice to finally realize your value? To belong someplace where nothing is required of you except a few heartfelt prayers and praise songs?

Holy Spirit is saying now, "you are not an orphan." You have a Father— a provider, a protector, a home. The Sisterhood is not just a place of refuge, but a movement to pervade our reality with enlightened activity, peace, and love of God. We are called to love and to seek God more than any abusers, to hold onto our devotion and let the rest go. The crossroad decision between old life and new hinges on one question: what or who do you love most?

"Oshun must be tethered to Yemaya."
— Dreamtime

The biggest trap for the divine feminine is Oshun's insatiable love. In our youth, as omo (children of) Oshun, we may mistake her love for the world as an excuse for our own materialistic excess. Her love can easily become whoredom, if left unchecked. For this reason, there should be no spiritual house where Oshun is the sole reigning Orisha in play. This, by the way, was a partial cause of my trouble with the sangoma teacher. She was still in her Oshun. Meanwhile I was phasing out of Oshun and into Oya/Yemaya. Add Orunmila/Isithunywa to the mix and we could only part ways.

At her best, Oshun has the gift of seeing sweetness where it may be lacking. She idealizes. Too often though it's her own wonderful self who gets the glory. She loves herself FIRST. Loves the physical first. At her worst, Oshun is acquisitive, egotistical, and conceited. I know this because I have Oshun. In full bloom on the darkside she hosts the Jezebel spirit. Jezebel is notorious in the Christian ethos for persecuting and killing prophets. The Word of God always effaces her unchecked ego. It's the nature of the Dharmakaya or AahUah as all pervading space vs. the nature of Qadesh or Adishakti as physical/birth-oriented/material existence. But, mind **is** over matter... There **is** a definite hierarchy here which must be respected and maintained. The feminine holds no divinity in and of itself. The Jezebel/dark Oshun individual will argue that she is a Goddess in her own right. But to that there is but one reply: Everything you give birth to dies. How divine can you be?

This isn't all just a hard pill to swallow for men who thought their phalluses were the font of life. No. The so-called divine feminine must eat her own slice of humble pie.

We must all be humble where truth is concerned. In a sense, everything here is feminine compared to the masculine nature of

61

God– as Krishna's famed devotee, Mirabai, so eloquently posited. The sweeter side of Oshun, the maiden, is deferential and submissive. Comparatively, focusing on Radha's seeking of Krishna is a powerful antidote to the darker tendencies of our feminine nature. And this is where Yemaya excels as a mentor for the child of Oshun because Yemaya has realized her function to be that of a mother. Any good mother is more focused on her children than on herself. So, she naturally self-negates. Tethered to Yemaya, Oshun can flower.

In Kemetic terms this is the relationship between the goddesses of Maat– HetHeru/Auset, Nebethet/Auset, aka Nephthys and Isis. It serves as the true foundation of our mystery school tradition. Look at the hieroglyphs and temple wall depictions again. Do you see it? They're partners.

Nebethet literally means "lordess of the house." Following Isis' example, she learns to mimic Yemaya in her peaceful state and Oya in her disciplinary fury. Together they fight for what is correct and maintain Maat in the household. The maiden Oshun benefits from this structure and because it is her life's breath as an initiate, she will respect it.

The union of Oshun and Orunmila is an even more fruitful bond which bears spiritual fruit. In fact, during my own growth into prophethood an omo Oshun hovered close to the ile (our spiritual house) eagerly soaking up whatever wisdom came through. And that's the major distinction, an Oshun bent on love of God is a truly beautiful thing. She keeps her own negative tendencies in check, as would any sincere initiate. Great Spirit was so impressed with this particular omo Oshun initiate that she eventually became my apetebi and co-wife of God... only according to Ifa's direction of course.

It's interesting to see here that it's entirely possible for a Yemaya or Oya individual to also be a prophet, crowned Orunmila. In that case, Ifa itself will call Oshun to serve as apetebi. An apetebi is first and foremost a wife of Ifa. She submits herself to Ifa willingly, in full acceptance of her call to serve in the priesthood. Oshun's loving, nurturing nature can flower accordingly, manifesting through the life-sustaining work of midwifery, pre- and post-partum doula care, herbalism and alternative medicine, gardening, childcare, education and so on. These are not chauvinistic impositions on a meek and enslaved womanhood, but viable tools to harness, feed, and explore our feminine nature. We are waterfalls walking. Such a feeding of the feminine leads to flowering for the entire society as a whole. Wherever women are happiest, everything fructifies.

This reminds me of something that Great Spirit revealed via dreamtime several years ago. There were cows walking in procession, in lines as far as my eyes could see. Some walked standing upright like humans, across a bridge, while others walked on four legs through the water below. All around was marshland and trees with hanging foliage. The meaning? We are reclaiming our place as the holy cow Goddess bearing God's manifestation– Hathor. HetHeru. We are the house of Heru. We are the waters of Mem, of Nun, from which Atum arises. To be a nun is to seek God fully without diversion, to seek Him with wholehearted devotion. This is the penultimate expression of the divine feminine.

What about the men? How can a man serve as a sun while respecting a woman's calling to serve as a nun? Let's address men specifically here, as inclusion is important. Men are not pariahs. The Great Oneness has revealed the important role men can play in this unfolding, through various wisdom texts. Both the masculine and the feminine and everything in between all have a blueprint for serving as living suns, as beni KaRaIst.

Love is a hoe. In ancient kemetic terms, love was represented by a glyph for this common garden tool. Depictions of men who served the deity Min can be seen chiseled into the temple walls. They appear decked out in formal regalia and carrying hoes. Meaning: to love is to cultivate, to till the ground– to prepare it for seed. As gardners, some men have a profound calling and responsibility to grow roses out of concrete. In this manner, they can still love women even if not impregnating us, if AahUah wills. They can uplift us and support us in various ways, while respecting our choice to either marry God or marry men. However, there must be no coercion.

In the section on Eve/Chava we discussed "doing it wrong." How we've been having too much sex, the wrong way. If we look forward in the Bible to Mary we see what it looks like to do things right. Mary restores what was broken. She recovers what was lost after humanity's fall into a dualistic hell realm. She demonstrates how we were originally designed to procreate with the Most High directly. So who stood by Mary and her equally miraculous cousin Elizabeth through the divine conception/divine birth process? According to biblical accounts– Joseph and Zacharia. Males.

Take with you seven pairs of every kind of clean animal, a male and its mate, and one pair of every kind of unclean animal, a male and its mate, and also seven pairs of every kind of bird, male and female, to keep their various kinds alive throughout the earth. —NIV

Of every behemah hatehorah thou shalt take to thee by sevens; the male and his mate; and of behemah that are not tehorah by two, the male and his mate. Of also Oph HaShomayim by sevens, the **zachar and the nekevah***; to keep zera (seed) alive upon the face of kol ha'aretz. —OJB*

Way before Mary turns things around through obedience, in Genesis 7 we see that God was sending a flood to destroy a sinful humanity. It's a humanity which had fallen far away from the non-dual oneness intended in Eden. We're nudged again and again to mend this rift, this dualism, through union. Most mercifully, YHWH warns His prophet—Noah— to build a huge ship, filling it with his family and pairs of animals two by two. Deep symbolic meaning here. This is a blueprint on how not to be swept away by the wages of sin, the flood of dualistic consequence.

If we look to the Hebrew translation, YHWH refers to these pairs as **zachar and nekevah**. Save the cheerleader, save the world. This zachar (zayin-kaph-resh or zkr) is zikr in the Muslim/Sufi world. This is the ritual chanting of God's names. When done right, it's trance inducing. The male YHWH is speaking of here is implored to lead the nekevah to Him! The male priest leads her to remembrance of God, to the chanting of His names.

Even in marriage where a man takes on the responsibility of headship, he must still acknowledge that God or Christ (or Allah or Olodumare, etc) is above his own head. He must demonstrate that he submits to God's authority. In Kemetic terms, zachar is Seker/Skr/Zkr– high priest, monk, renunciate devotee. Seker is a master at the utterance of heka, mantra, and wielding spiritual power through discipline and asceticism. This is reminiscent of the Orunmila+apetebi dynamic of Ifa, though with more of an Orun twinge. Seker resonates with funerary mysteries, in the neighborhood of Shiva, Kali and the like. This is a person who has surrendered to God so completely that the world has been given up. Graveyards. Ecstatic tantric rites. Baron Samedi vibrations. This is definitely Saturn territory. From this place of discipline and religious devotion, the "zachar" priest of the home can lead his "nekevah" wife.

Nekevah refers to Nekhebet, the totemic form of Nebethet– the "lordess of the house" in Kemetic tradition. She is "Rabbaitul Bait" in Islam. Where Seker represents dying to self and a mastery of chanting, Nekhebet/Nebethet was similarly known as a goddess of death. As Nekhebet, her emblem is the vulture. As Nebethet, her emblems are a house and a basket, an acquisitive material nature. Temporality. Perishability. She is as Maman Brigit to Baron Samedi. In Kemetic lore, Nebethet was actually married to Set, the closest approximation to the devil in ancient Egyptian terms. Though married to Set, Nebethet went to bed with Asar/Osiris and conceived a son, Anpu/Anubis. Again we have a mother of dead things– like Chava. Where Nebethet had intercourse with men (her husband Set and an affair with Ausar), Aset/Isis on the other hand did not. Rather,

Aset served as God's throne and maintained devotion to Him even after his death.

So let's unmuddy these complicated waters. **Before** Mary, marriage between male and female was the way (i.e. Genesis 7). Before Aset's devotion, the woman of the house laid with her lord and apparently other women's lords. But because of Mary's obedience and willingness to receive whatever God had for her, she broke the curse. Death and duality were destroyed. Aset, likewise, reestablished God's kingdom by birthing his heir and breaking the curse of Set's evil vindictive reign.

Notice too that Zachariah's wife was barren, he couldn't have a child though he longed to. So he prayed to God who eventually sent Gabriel with the good news: By the will of YHWH, his wife Elizabeth would conceive. God intervened and took over the womb of both these women, Mary and Elizabeth.

Note also that the priest Zachariah (father of John the Baptist via divine conception) was rendered mute by Archangel Gabriel because he did not believe God's word, God's promise regarding conception. A demonstration of zikr, priestly utterance, without power– rather than faith in God the man was filled with doubt (Luke 1:8-20).

There is so much to unpack in all of these mysteries and names, but the paramount message is this: chant God's names to be safe from the flood. Listen to your heart and choose to be a wife of God or a wife of man… "The way is through love."

The Non-Dual Emptiness of Maat

*"I have more to say to you, more than you can now bear. But when he, the
Spirit of Truth, comes, he will guide you into all the truth."*
John 16:12-13 NIV

The ankh symbol is a key to unlocking these mysteries for
oneself. Being told by someone only scratches the surface,
prepares the ground so to speak, but direct revelation and
experience will give confirmation of this word.

Shen, in Kemetic terms, is the open space comprising the
top portion of the ankh. It means "eternity." This open space is
feminine in nature. The womb assures the preservation of our
species. Continuity. Seen also as the Kaaba, in Makkah, this open
space exerts an almost gravitational pull. Magnetic. Attractive.
On the Kaaba we see what appears to be a vulva and a door. The
divine feminine is a door to God. Allah, aka Al Ilah aka The
God, exists in full limitless expanse on the other side of the
female door. AahUah is a non-dual being manifesting into
physical form through the feminine form of Oneness: AahUat.

In tantric terms, one is instructed to gaze upon the secret
lotus face of a woman to attain the fruit of meditation. One must
go through the door, mentally, to get to God. In Ifa terms, Eshu
Eleggua opens the way. If one is fortunate enough to have the
gate opened, one can get absorbed in that unlimited expanse.
Such is the power, beauty and purpose of a woman's holy door.

The shen does not stand alone however. The masculine is
represented beneath it, together forming an ankh. This ankh

symbolizes "life." So often I've heard that it represents balance, specifically the balance of man and woman... union of man and woman, producing children. However, that is incorrect. The ankh is a symbol of androgyny. The balance it points to is complete within one being– both the masculine and feminine aspects of one's nature in harmonious accord. There is no separation. There is no need to seek balance outside oneself by seeking a partner of the opposite sex. To do so actually brings death. The life which is produced is only temporary. We've been practicing, playing with the ideas of duality, union, and balance. Now we're called to finally graduate into full blown gnosis.

Beyond the forms and dogmas of the various world religions we have an all pervasive truth: life springs from the union of masculine and feminine. If we simply shift our focus from gross physical expression to higher subtle expression we can realize this great mystic union in this very lifetime.

"But when that One has come, the Ruach Hakodesh, the Ruach HaEmes,
He will guide you in all truth."
John 16:12-13 OJB

In the book of John, Yeshua tells us that Ruach Hakodesh, Ruach HaEmes, will come to guide the world into the truth. Ruach is the essence (ashé/aché) of the Father
(Ru or Ra + aché; Kemetic/Yoruba). When this "Holy Spirit" came to me in dreamtime, He said "Look to the soul word of your Fathers." He used the term Ru. Heru/Horus also refers to this aché of the Father. Don't let anyone take your Father God from you. Each one of us has a direct connection and He will come to those who are sincere.

Furthermore, He isn't coming alone. Ruach is coming with Emet/Emes. On seeing this word, Emet, Great Spirit immediately revealed Maat to my inner ear. Emet = Truth. With no vowels this is M+T. In ancient Kemetic terms, Maat is the spirit of truth– And Maat is a woman. As Sebai Muata Ashby perfectly elucidates in the *Prt m Heru* (aka *The Egyptian Book of Coming Forth by Day*):

> "Who are the Maati Goddesses? In the segment above we introduced the idea of opposites in creation. The Hall of Maat, known as the hall of judgment for the heart, is presided over by the two goddesses known as Maati. The goddesses Aset and Nebethet have a special relationship to the Maati goddesses. The ancient Egyptian texts reveal that these two goddesses are none other than Aset and Nebethet..." Pg 96

So Ruach Hakodesh, aka Holy Spirit, is flanked by two goddesses who represent the Truth. On the walls of our ancient Kemetic temples we can still see depictions of Ausar/Osiris flanked by these two goddesses. M+T of the words Emet and Maat also bring to mind Mut which means mother. Mut– the vulture goddess who is associated with divine kingship.

We can follow the trail of our vulture mother to Ifa, where Oshun flew up to heaven as a peacock and lost all of her beautiful feathers, becoming a vulture. She did this in order to save the world, to reach Olodumare/God on behalf of the Orishas and humanity. Oshun did this to end famine, disease and death. She sacrificed her own ego, her beauty, her wants and so on... to pursue God and bring His blessings back to the Earth.

70

God is calling us to this mystery of Maat and non-dual union now. Rather than perpetuating the man plus woman dynamic, we are being called to embody the union of Nebethet and Aset, maintaining the House of Heru. This is Aset, the Throne of God.

Men are being called to assist and to lay down any man child on the altar of AahUah– dedicated to His purposes. God is the Alpha and Omega, the beginning and the end. Every knee shall bow.

Alpha = Aleph, the first letter, Bull/Ox head.
Omega = Shen/top of the ankh, last letter greek alphabet.
Tav = Crossed sticks, last letter hebrew alphabet.

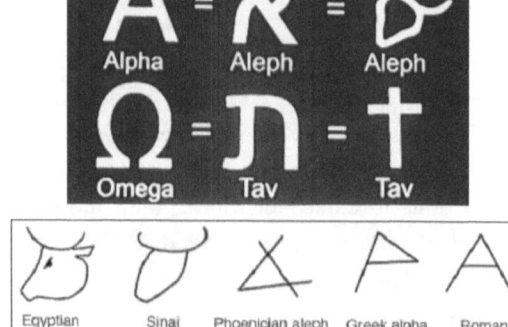

Tav

Early Hebrew	Middle Hebrew	Late Hebrew	Modern Hebrew
✝	✕	𝔫	ת

Ancient Name: Taw
Pictograph: Crossed Sticks
Meanings: Mark, Sign, Signal, Monument
Sound: T

"I am the Alpha (Aleph) and the Omega (Tav), the First and the
Last, the Beginning and the End."
Revelation 22:13

The Great Bull of His Mother, KaMutef, was propitiated in
ancient Kemet. The bull was sacrificed religiously, just as Yeshua
was sacrificed. The king serves The Great Oneness and is
cautioned again and again, across various cultural-mythological
stages, not to act selfishly, not to wield power as a tyrant. Yeshua,
the Christ, is our penultimate example of the ideal, a
self-sacrificing king. Yeshua always pointed to His Father in
heaven, even while driving home the fact that, "I and the Father
are One."

So we have been shown the beginning and the end. It all began with God/Yah/the Great Bull/Ausar and He is preparing to finish it, with His shen… His bride, His womb of millions of years. We are His holy house. Matter/Mother is the holy house of Spirit/Father. And when He comes down into physicality He exhibits love for His creation even to the point of self-sacrificing death.

The first (Alpha/Aleph/male principle) will be last and the last (Omega/Shen/female principle) will be first. The throne of God will be established on Earth with Aset/Isis in a divinely ordained Maatriarchy. The masculine abdicates this earthly throne of power (i.e. Christ's crucifixion, Abraham's offering of Issac). In spirit the masculine is exalted, as the all seeing eye, as the supreme Dharmakaya, as Amun Ra etc. The masculine rules/predominates in the mental/spiritual sphere while the feminine rules/predominates in the emotional/physical sphere. Through zikr (Seker in ancient Kemet), both male and female attain balance, gnosis– through never ceasing remembrance of God.

Everything born of man dies. Everything born of woman also dies… unless that being is seeded by the Ruach of Father God Himself. Let us all come into heartfelt remembrance.

There's so much symbolism in this one infamous sentence… The last will be first and the first will be last (Matthew 20:16). AUM also contains the truth of the Alpha and Omega. See it? Aleph/Alpha is first and UM/OM is last. Or, in its extreme termination, M is last. So, here, we're being shown that Shiva's domain of destruction and dissolution –the void, the nothing– will be first… perhaps even just for an instant. A new creation will be the result, thus making the A last. Could it be that, rather than the violent hellfire we expected, we instead choose to bring about a planet wide reset of our own volition? Buddhas appearing across the globe in all directions in simultaneous self-realization? Everyone at peace, no longer fighting over or fighting against a misperceived God?

It dawned on me along this most recent leg of my spiritual journey that the Bible was written by rishis. Had to have been. As my mother used to say, "a little birdie told me." Yet, I was amazed to actually find the term Rishonim in the text while exploring Alpha and Omega…

> Rishonim: first ones (i.e. Rishis). A Rishi is a great sage. An accomplished/enlightened person
> (courtesy: Wikipedia).
>
> Acharonim: last ones (i.e. Acharyas) An Acharya is a great teacher who leads by example, by their conduct (courtesy Yogapedia). Gurus, teachers of yoga and religion.

The rishis knew the end from the onset– it ends how it began. The acharonim are ultimately becoming rishis themselves. It seems that was always the intention of the wise ones and of God… even from the very first biblical line: "In the beginning…"

Even if you're on the fence about God, surely it makes sense that there would be spiritually advanced individuals influencing the course of human history. That's something one can have faith in, if nothing else. And unless the heart has become hardened, one can imagine noble intentions at play, on the part of such rishis and saints. Rather than having bleak motives of trapping souls in samsara, enlightened beings are notorious for seeking enlightenment and liberation for all sentient beings.

If you rise to become a rishi, or buddha or what have you… what would **you** do? How would you help humanity? Rather than being mad at "creator" we are being ushered into knowledge of how to play the game… to win, and to become game designers ourselves. Visualizing higher lokas and buddha realms is a key facet of meditation practice.

It begins with making the vows of a bodhisattva. It starts with serving and helping AahUah's people from a place of emptiness, peace, and Maat.

Amakhosi Masks: Spheres of the Neteru

Without the work of my predecessors I may well have remained in the dark for many more years. I don't believe these epiphanies would have come to me so easily without the groundwork laid through studying their work. Gratitude to Sebai Dr. Muata Ashby and his wife & to Shekem ur Shekem Ra Un Nefer Amen and his wives. Their spiritual genius and scholarly contribution to the fields of African Traditional Religion and metaphysics in general is unparalleled.

The framework of the Tree of Life and the explanation of the Neteru, spiritual archetypes, helped me understand my own nature and proceed along the path without getting confounded. I was able to categorize other people's behavior based on the tree, and alter my own behavior/expectations accordingly. Knowing who you are and who you're dealing with is half the battle. So before I share this template I want to say thank you to these two spiritual giants. Thokoza, Dua, Mojuba, and Pranam to your Kas.

We've had enough complexity. While studying the Tree of Life can be complex and multilayered, especially when compared with the Kabbalah, I'm going to present it as simply as possible so it can be used as a tool by any seeker. This is a method which has worked for me.

Whenever you get stuck or find yourself experiencing challenges at a certain sphere of the Tree, focus on one question: How do I ground these energies to manifest the ideal? This is accomplished by finding the complementary sphere to equal 10 (Geb/manifestation) or to equal 0 (transcendence).

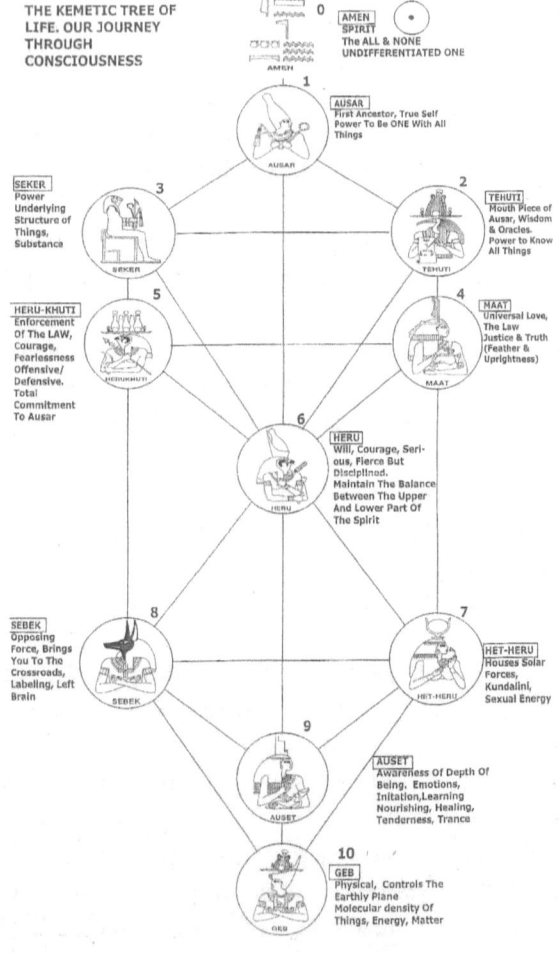

THE KEMETIC TREE OF LIFE. OUR JOURNEY THROUGH CONSCIOUSNESS

0 AMEN SPIRIT The ALL & NONE UNDIFFERENTIATED ONE

1 AUSAR First Ancestor, True Self Power To Be ONE With All Things

3 SEKER Power Underlying Structure of Things, Substance

2 TEHUTI Mouth Piece of Ausar, Wisdom & Oracles. Power to Know All Things

5 HERU-KHUTI Enforcement Of The LAW, Courage, Fearlessness Offensive/ Defensive. Total Commitment To Ausar

4 MAAT Universal Love, The Law Justice & Truth (Feather & Uprightness)

6 HERU Will, Courage, Serious, Fierce But Disciplined. Maintain The Balance Between The Upper And Lower Part Of The Spirit

8 SEBEK Opposing Force, Brings You To The Crossroads, Labeling, Left Brain

7 HET-HERU Houses Solar Forces, Kundalini, Sexual Energy

9 AUSET Awareness Of Depth Of Being. Emotions, Initiation, Learning Nourishing, Healing, Tenderness, Trance

10 GEB Physical, Controls The Earthly Plane Molecular density Of Things, Energy, Matter

For example, say a sister is stuck on the negative side of sphere 7, in extreme lust and materialistic pleasure. Which complementary sphere would bring balance & grounding, helping her to manifest the ideal? $7 + 3 = 10$. So it is Seker at sphere 3 which would remedy this imbalance. Chanting/remembering God's names, building spiritual power through self-discipline, auterities, tapasaya, etc. This focus counteracts the deleterious effects of squandering sexual arousal and being overly preoccupied with material enjoyments. Sphere 7's Venusian Oshun energy is balanced and corrected through Saturn's influence at sphere 3. This is also a perfect demonstration of the apetebi+Orunmila dynamic. One would of course need to study these spheres and spiritual influences in greater detail to master their skillful application. But for starters, know that such a practice is not about offering candles and food to "gods," graven images and such, but rather knowing how to shift and phase through the various aspects of one's own nature (aka Ntr).

And, alternatively, perhaps the sister experiencing troubles with sphere 7 is nowhere near a Seker/priestly type or completely unaware of what to do exactly... If she is so inclined she can apply the opposite equation: $7-7=0$. As Sadhguru has so categorically reminded us, "I am not the body, I am not even the mind." There is no duality. So, no longer see any separation. It's a conscious choice. In this zero place of unconditioned responses and desires, identifying with no learned personality traits, one can simply detach from the Oshun/Venusian personality construct altogether. Ideally, the detachment is achieved via meditation then applied tangibly in relationships and life choices. It's very simple math, but completely life altering when carried out diligently.

Another example. Say someone is stuck at sphere 8, Sebek/Mercury, with too much reliance on logic, reason and cunning. Overthinking is a prison of its own. 8+2=10. So the person would benefit from incorporating the gifts of Tehuti/Thoth: wisdom, theoretical conceptualization, spiritual truth. Entheogenes may also help in shifting awareness from logical thoughts to more creative, dream-oriented thoughts and visions– under proper shamanic supervision. Tehuti's creative, artistic, holistic and congregative way of thinking, based on wisdom, would be key to push beyond any segregative, analytical, linear thinking which understands by separating things into compartments.* Instead, through the higher wisdom represented by Jupiter, a person would be able to understand based on the bigger picture and an interconnectivity with all. Maat is also related to Tehuti and Jupiter, so high spiritual truth, proverbs, the wisdom of the sages and so on would help resolve any shortcomings of an unbalanced sphere 8. Divine law and truth take precedence over man made laws, rules, and limited perceptions. The wellbeing of the whole supersedes the cunning desires of one in isolation. This we learn by balancing spheres 8 and 2.

Note that if someone presents with imbalances at sphere 5, great care is needed. It cannot be paired with any other number to equal 10. It stands alone. At worst, such an individual may have a strong egoic sense of self importance or a desire for war which perceives everyone as an enemy. Hotheaded. Disagreeable.

---

*See *Medu Neter* by Ra Un Nefer Amen for further exploration of spiritual development in light of brain hemisphere orientation.

Resistant to empathy. A "my way or the highway" kind of person. Herukhuti/Ogun/Mars stands unopposed. There is no direct counterbalance. Ideally, this person serves Maat or Ifa and Ausar or Obatala so that justice can manifest where God's divine order is concerned. But, if personal ego is clouding perception of divine will, allowing personal limited will to dominate, then a 5 imbalance becomes dangerous beyond measure. Severity must be balanced with mercy. Across from Mars/Herukhuti on the Tree sits Jupiter/Maat. It's the closest, and therefore most relevant sphere to the sphere 5 person. Maat is the one thing which can pull such an individual back from the brink of madness and destruction. But be mindful, Ifa warns that a bloodthursty Ogun is even capable of raping his own mother, Yemaya. So it's best to anchor the sphere 5 person in Maat or Ifa or some system of high morality and spiritual truth long before adulthood. Of course, all society would benefit from such a spiritual anchor.

Ideally, Mars at sphere 5 is a protector and defender of Maat to its right and of Heru below. Heru at sphere 6, represented by the sun, is the place of God's divinely appointed leadership. The Pharaoh– Per Aah. Great House. When tethered to such a righteous and just authority figure, Herukhuti/Ogun/Mars can simply follow orders, doing what needs to be done for the sake of the Kingdom or society. Iron can destroy, as a weapon, or serve as load bearing support.

An additional case: Say a sister is stuck at sphere 9, with submissive moon energetics, devoted to the wrong people or the wrong things. Such a female may easily become depleted as she gives all her energy out and receives nothing in return or at worst becomes a victim of abuse. Who and what should a sphere 9

Aset/Isis/Yemaya type person be devoted to? 9+1=10. Ausar at the top of the Tree is her direct complement. If ever she is feeling anxiety, fear, or some other emotion which threatens to handicap her she has one primary recourse: her true husband. All she needs to do is remember Him, channel Him, and be in His presence. It's like a major cheat, or easter egg, in a video game. She has a direct route, bypassing all the other spheres. Dua Hemut Amun!

This game of spheres could go on ad infinitum. It's fun and satisfying to play with the possibilities. This, by the way, is why it's so easy for us to get stuck playing with our idols. We must always remember that these spheres are like masks. We apply whichever sphere is required to accomplish whatever goal presents itself. We learn and apply whichever deific traits prove efficacious. But never do we permanently identify with any such mask or deific form.

Sun Worshipers

"I pay homage to the awakening sun, the sunrise. I pay homage to the dying sun, the sunset. I pay homage to the sun. I pay homage to the moon... I pay homage to the stone of heaven, the immovable stone of Olodumare. I honor the strength of the stone and the mystery of the stone of creation..." *

"Whenever the sun rises, it will rise for the whole world. There is nothing that can overpower the rising of the sun..."**

Ifa prayers

Spiritual pursuit of God, gnosis, and so on is not only about attaining for one's own sake. In attaining, one crosses the threshold of localized selfhood into greater perception of the Self as All. Bodhichitta naturally expresses. In Kemetic terms one attains nehast and is maakheru– awake and true of speech with spiritual power to effect the manifested construct, for the sake of all sentient beings. One goes from obscuration to a clear and perfected mind, vast and empty like the sky. Within that expanse, the sun, aka Ra, burns unceasingly.

The term AUM/OM which we're so familiar with holds additional significance if we look to the hieratic and hieroglyphic script of ancient Kemet...

---

*Courtesy: *The Diloggun* by Ocha'Ni Lele. **As taught by Baba Ifabayo, Nigeria.

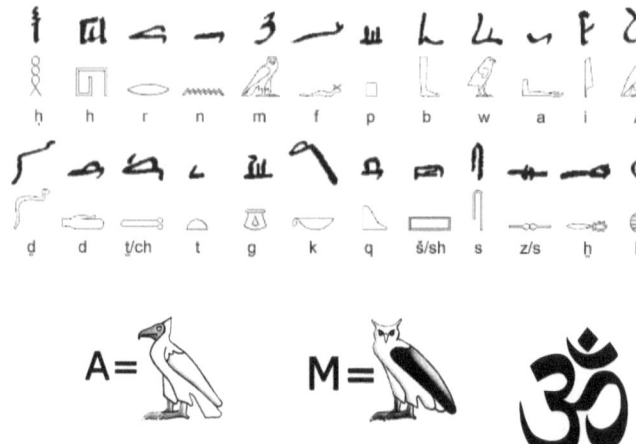

Clearly the sagacious rishis/seba priests responsible for the revelation of this mantra were demonstrating a big truth through its combination of letters. In the beginning God created everything and separated the light from the darkness, the day from the night (see Genesis 1). The owl is a bird of night while the vulture dominates during the day, assimilating the death. Night/Moon is counterbalanced by Day/Sun. The A signifies waking creation while the M signifies deep dreamless sleep.

Furthermore, the vulture, or Mother Goddess as Nekhebet, had one primary purpose: to resurrect the King. The King sailed in His solar barque in the duat, in the astral planes, according to His merit and degree of awake-ness/nehast. If He proved to be justified and righteous –maakheru– this regent would rise again after death to sit on the throne in a position of leadership as a form of Ra.

There is much more to the mystery, to be sought through proper initiation, but even upon rudimentary reflection it should be perfectly clear– our ancient Egyptian ancestors were not just some simple-minded pagan worshipers of the sun. Rather, they understood that there is a hierarchy, an order to creation. They followed the sun's path as it trailed its way through nighttime darkness in anticipation of its return. In our manifested construct, the sun serves as the central pivot point with all the other planets revolving around it. Our sun burns with power and energy, emitting life generating rays.

It's a well known fact among experts on ancient Egyptian culture that the pharaoh was often called a "son of Ra." Religious culture and state culture revolved around the linchpin of righteous leadership. This brings to mind the biblical quotation of YHWH regarding Yeshua: "This is my son in whom I am well pleased." However, resisting the urge to swallow the meaning we've been taught affords us a great and actionable revelation:

Matthew 3:17
English: "This is my <u>son</u> in whom I am well pleased."
Hebrew: ZEH <u>BNI</u> AHUVI ASHER BO CHAFATZTI
Corrected:
seed <u>house of nun</u>, beloved of Asr, well pleased/hasten

Proponents of Islam have adamantly pointed out that Allah refutes this statement in the Quran:

> Those who say: 'The Lord of Mercy has begotten a son,' preach a monstrous falsehood, at which the very heavens might crack, the earth break asunder, and the

mountains crumble to dust. That they should ascribe a
son to the Merciful, when it does not become the Lord
of Mercy to beget one!

—Quran Surah Maryam 19:88

On one level we could say this Quran verse signifies God's
nature as Brahman, THE absolute all pervasive being-ness with
no trace of separation— having no other, no second, no thing
apart from it in creation. It's the way an advanced yogi may
speak, i.e. Avadhuta Gita or Ashtavakra Gita. Also evident when
Yeshua asked rhetorically, "Who is my mother, and who are my
brothers?" Yeshua then points to his disciples and calls them his
mother and brothers (Matthew 12:46-50). The point is to resist
identification with the limitations of form, identification with
roles and identities.

To understand this "God's son" refutation from another
angle we must analyze the term BNI or ben, which we're told
means son in Hebrew. This is what YahUah is actually well
pleased with and calls us to hasten to…

B = bet = house
N = nun = sprouting seed, heir, perpetuation
Nun in Kemetic terms = waters/woman

ב Beit	**א** Alef	Av (Hebrew) **Father**
ן Nun	**ב** Beit	Ben (Hebrew) **Son**
ן Nun	**ב** Beit	**א** Alef	Even (Hebrew) **Stone**

Abn = Stone/Rock

Matthew 16:18
NIV Translation: And I tell you that you are Peter, and on this rock I will build my church, and the gates of Hades will not overcome it.

Orthodox Hebrew: And I also say to you that you are Shimon **Kefa** [Petros] and upon this **TSUR** I will build my **Kehillah**, my Chavurah (the Community of Moshiach) and the shaarei Sheol (gates of Sheol) shall not overpower it.

Word Play:
Lailah = night in Hebrew
La ilah = "the God" in Arabic
Kahf = cave, i.e. hollow stone, hollow rock
Kallah = bride
Kehillah = community

So the rock upon which YahUah will build His church?
A house of nuns: the cave-rock-bride of the God.

BEN doesn't literally mean son, rather
it demonstrates the means to produce him. The word points to
the house of Heru, HetHeru/Nebethet. The rock is what we
have when God Himself dwells in said house...

In the word for rock, ABN, Aleph of course represents God as a
Bull in Hebrew. Also we have the Kemetic aspect in which the A
points to the work of Mut, the vulture mother Nekhebet. She
leads the brides of God, as seen in the Kemetic hieratic AUM.

> Moving now to the word "kallah," we are also unsure as
> to its origin. As in the case of chatan, we are faced with
> two meanings, "bride" and "daughter-in-law," and we
> are not sure which was primary.
>
> Some point to an Akkadian verb K-L-L that meant "to
> conceal the face or head," which could have developed
> into a word for "bride," due to the bridal veil. Others
> point to an Akkadian verb K-L-L that meant "to
> crown." There was also a similar-sounding noun in
> Akkadian for crown. Perhaps, it is argued, Hebrew
> once had such words. (The Akkadian verb and noun
> for crown seems to be the source for the post-biblical
> Hebrew word for crown: "kelil," and its Aramaic
> equivalent: "kelila.") Alternatively, some speculate that
> "kallah" means "bride" based on the Hebrew root
> kaph-lamed-aleph, which meant something like

"closed." <u>The kallah is one who is closed off to the world, except to her husband.</u>
{Source:
jewishlink.news/features/19830-what-is-the-origin-of-the-words-chatan-and-kallah}

In Matthew 3:17 we have the Great Oneness declaring His pleasure not just in His offspring but in His house of nuns. He makes it clear that it pleases Him that He seeds His nuns– those beloved ones of Asar. And who does Asar love? Who flanks Him as He sits on the throne? Aset and Nebethet, aka Maat. So it is woman (nun) who is the "ahuvi" or beloved of God. Woman who was/is supposed to sit on the throne of her Lord, exalting Him through righteous leadership of His great house of nuns.

Nun

Early Hebrew	Middle Hebrew	Late Hebrew	Modern Hebrew

Ancient Name: Nun
Pictograph: Sprouting Seed
Meanings: Continue, Heir, Son
Sound: N

History & Reconstruction

The ancient pictograph  is a picture of a seed sprout representing the idea of continuing to a new generation. This pictograph has the meanings of "continue," "perpetuation," "offspring" and "heir."

Nun in Kemetic Glyphs

As women bent on manifesting the divine feminine we priestesses are admonished to do the work of the mother goddess Nebethet/HetHeru/Aset. This is wakefulness. We are implored to make it through the night, deciphering and following our dreams, in order to do the work of supporting, maintaining and embodying Maat in service of Amun Ra, in service of the Great Oneness.

Back to Alpha and Omega. As far as the last being first, we are already in the dark. It's already been owl season, hasn't it? We've been perpetuating Eve's sin outside of Maat. We are now going from darkness to light, from M to A, from Omega to Alpha. It's true what brother James said in the Bible, faith without works is dead (James 2:26). If we do not do the actual work of Nebethet/HetHeru, the Aset throne of God, we are dooming the planet to dualistic darkness and spiritual apathy. It's not enough to just "believe in God." It has never been enough. We must manifest God and make the offerings.

Even with this great passage of time– the Exodus and the Maafa, the Holocaust, the jihads, the crusades, the Apartheid– God is still God. No matter the apparent devastation wrought by enslavement, religious or social persecution, colonization, and the like, no one can take God from you. No one can take God from any people. We must each aspire to know Him for ourselves. He can be found within and without, according to how spiritually advanced any given society is.

All we need do is look to see if any given society is revolving around leadership which is maakheru in nehast. Whether such societies or communities contain a womanhood which flowers, as nuns, within sacred enclosure. The women who answer this call must be set apart and safe– unmolested and undisturbed. Such societies will undoubtedly possess women and men alike who serve as living suns, bringing light and truth and sustenance to all.

This is our work, as a world priesthood. As suns of AahUah we must manifest God and make the offerings– offering education and healthcare, housing and spiritual instruction. Righteous leadership offers bread to the thirsty, housing to the homeless, and a boat to the shipwrecked (Husia*). In this way one becomes an acharya or ultimately a rishi. In this way one becomes a PerAah/Pharaoh. In this way one becomes beloved of Ra, walking as a living sun.

---

*Courtesy: "Selections from the Huisa," Maulana Karenga.

ODUDUWA

How does one know who is a sun– who is worthy of serving or aligning with? Ifa gives us a framework. We serve Oduduwa, the divinely appointed leader of the house or society. This appellation references the office of THE great monarch who established the first holy city of *Ile Ife. Its colors–that of a PerAah–are white, green, and a little red. The white symbolizes Olodumare/God, the green symbolizes the prophet Orunmila/Isithunywa, while the red symbolizes Shango/iShaka– aka kingship. Called Oduduwa, or PerAah, or Khosi Amakhosi for example, this individual represents all three of these roles in one being.

Because the red is "small small" we are reminded that any monarch, or local regent, is small in relation to God and the prophets. The regent's ego must always be in check, subservient to Maat. She/He/They must always submit to God's will as spoken by any true prophet, by Ifa, or whichever means AahUah chooses to send Word.

So for the sake of Maat we are behooved to hold the keepers of the throne, any Oduduwas, in high regard. Also, consequently, omo Obatala, omo Olokun, any prophets, and any righteous leaders should be greatly respected and supported. Eshu Eleggua must also be given his due respect, naturally, as Lord of the crossroads. The rest fall into order around this central axis. We are thus given a focal point for our efforts as a society. Of course

---

*Respect also to Benin/Tado, my ancestral land, & to the Fulani.

THE God itself, in this case termed Olodumare, is without a partner– omnipotent, omniscient, and omnipresent. All bow before the authority of this Great Oneness, the Owner of Everything.

The temple structure of ancient Kemet was based on such a systematic organization of focus resulting in purposeful effort. In this way, our world can be filled with buddha activity. As the wise Confucius demonstrated, with his systematic appointing of age-based-responsibilities, such order allows society to flourish because everyone knows where they belong in the flow of things. On the other hand, we must not allow strict caste systems to develop which threaten creativity and basic human rights.

It's gratifying to conjecture on the flowering of human potential which is possible in such a society. But we must maintain our tether to God's will. This requires a high level of maturity on the part of the people. Can you, as an individual, submit yourself to what's right? Can you place your own personal egoic desires on the back burner for the sake of what's beneficial for the whole? I wonder if we're capable and ready to be a world society which serves one common purpose– Maat, the truth of Oneness resulting in social harmony. Certainly I hope so. But I know firsthand what it means to submit to higher truth, that's the fruit of any true initiation. We must each allow such a refining of our natures.

Let us not get hung up on cultural labels in the process. Maat shouldn't be conceived of as a foreign ethos which must completely overwrite and stamp out any current culture. Rather, Maat can be integrated, interwoven into the already existing social fabric. These principles can and should be taught to both young and old. If the young, especially, receive right education from the beginning of their development, society would be spared the backlash of unchecked egotism when they reach adulthood. Reading the news headlines now affords us ample examples of school shootings and other public displays of rage which could have been prevented through right education. In school, I don't recall being taught any system of ethics or high morality. I had to study these for myself. Somehow, in America, we've come to accept a separation between church and state which leaves the people dying of thirst for real meaning and mystic experience.

To teach high morality and spiritual ethics in schools does not require that we beat our children over the head with dogma from any one religion. To the contrary, it would be most fruitful to teach ALL of the religions and spiritual frameworks which prove our world to be a place of righteous order and beauty.

Rather than teach our children nothing, let us teach them *everything.* We are too grown, as a planet, too rich with vast cultural expression, to deny our children the wisdom we have gained. I can imagine schools becoming hubs of great philosophical discourse. In Nigeria, for example, even elementary school children learn the patakis of Ifa. Can you imagine the wealth of creative genius we'll yield if our children learn Ifa, Sufi zikrs, the Shema Israel prayer, Zen koans, the Vedas, the way of the Bodhisattva, I-Ching, Runic wisdom, and Native American shamanism... simultaneously? Instead of dwelling on what makes each culture so different, we should be learning what we have in common. In this way, we cross a polytheistic bridge of another sort.

Another issue which may be contributing to the apathy or outright rage plaguing our society today is too much dependency on a mechanized way of life. City living has its advantages, but also its downsides. Cities serve as melting pots, so to speak, allowing the intermingling of diverse cultures. Yet, we're seeing rage burst open as violent prejudice– at churches, mosques, schools and so on. Cities foster a way of life which too often takes us away from cohesion with the natural world around us. What other result can we expect from a psyche which feels hemmed in by concrete, lack of employment and escalating expenses amid foreigners who "steal the jobs" or "threaten **our** values?" This scenario begs for disaster. It's imperative that we implement Maat and world philosophies into our school systems so that people are equipped with an ability to think outside their boxes– so that children don't grow to become adults who fear and hate. It's not good enough for us to believe in high morality/God as an abstract. We must manifest and make the offerings.

How do we start? Integrating more dependency on the natural world along with high moral principles from across cultural boundaries will spawn a more empathic humanity– a humanity which naturally and comfortably settles into The Way. The epitome of all our religious traditions is to not need to cling to them through labels but float in their headspace of peace and devotion. As Yeshua said, he did not come to negate the law but to fulfill it. It's go time. Time to manifest the ideals latent within our seemingly disparate traditions. They are not in fact separate.

> *"I do not go and seek the youthful and inexperienced, but he/she/they come and seek me. When that one shows the sincerity that marks the first recourse to divination, I instruct him/her/them. If that one applies a second and third time, that*

is troublesome; and I do not instruct the troublesome. There will be advantage in being firm and correct."
—*IChing Hexagram: IV Mang*

A hallmark of any rich ethical tradition is respect for righteous authority and rank, according to personal effort, ability and sincerity. We are reminded via this randomly selected hexagram to hold fast to the hierarchy of wisdom and experience. Today we too often heed voices who have nothing to offer but ego, attitude, and inexperience. In this we see the beauty of the initiation process, especially the mystery tradition system of ancient Kemet and the still prevalent ritual processes of Confucius. Everyday life itself is consequently made holy. We must deliberately make it so.

Ritual Meditation: Tea Ceremony

Supplies:

White candle

Incense

Special tea set

Bell

42 Declarations of Maat printed

Holy books from various cultures

Mystic poetry books

A mat or prayer rug

A tray or table to hold the materials

A bowl of water

- ❖ Come to kneeling then clean yourself using the water. Repeat, "I am pure, my heart is pure" three times (or whatever comes from your heart) while rubbing some of the water down your arms, on the back of your neck, down your front and back, down your thighs, legs and feet. Then sprinkle some water around the area.
- ❖ Ring the bell three times then say God's names.
- ❖ Pour the tea, preparing to taste, doing everything slowly and deliberately. Sip intermittently for the remainder.
- ❖ Recite the 42 Declarations of Maat aloud.
- ❖ Read quietly from a holy book.
- ❖ Spend some time in quiet reflection, considering areas in which you could improve and areas in which you are excelling in application of empathy, morality, and bodhicitta.
- ❖ Sing or chant mantras in praise of the Great Oneness/God
- ❖ Read from a sacred text, mystic poetry, etc.
- ❖ Bow when complete then extinguish the candle without blowing it out.

This tea ceremony is non-denominational/all-denominational. Incorporate wisdom texts from a broad array of theologies, philosophies and spiritual systems for maximum benefit. Anchor yourself in the works of the prophets. We follow the prophets and submit to the Great Oneness.

Let this centering become your resting position, the place you come back to regardless of what life throws at you. Carry the peace from this simple ceremony within you as you go about your day.

In Summary

Through Oduduwa, AahUah offers us an opportunity to fill our world with a new breed of humanity, simultaneously divine and human– the original plan. High morality, spiritual ethics, mystic union with the All.

Furthermore, this name–**Oduduwa**–contains a profound meaning: **Womb-Black-Ours**… Odu-Dudu-Wa.
You could also say: **Womb-Black-Oneness**…Odu-Dudu-Uah.

The Black Womb of AahUah.
The dark night sky of Nut through which Ra travels.
The waters of Nun which give birth to Atum.
It is the mystery of the Buddhist Dorje and Bell.
This is the living manifestation of the Kaaba, the womb of Auset/Mary, and the life-generating emptiness of the Ankh. This is the true dharma pervading our planet, latent,
and ready to birth.

Dua Tepi Ankh. Adorations to the Time of Life.
May all who walk in Maat enjoy Ankh n Heh…
Immortality, Eternal Life.
There is no God but God. There is ONLY God,
and I am one who has submitted.

How to Start a Sisterhood

If you're looking to start your own spiritual house, a sisterhood, you'll have to have your own God-given epiphanies. It's a calling. This text is a blueprint but you'll have to chop your own lumber. If it's meant to be, the Great Oneness will provide what's needed.

Anyone who initiates into this particular sorority– our House of the Leopard– of course is provided with hand holding and a jump start. It's helpful to have support through any personal shadow work– support in crossing that polytheistic bridge. This has notoriously been the work of the guru, the enlightened teacher who has already completed the process and now bears light to share. The Great Oneness is manifesting more female buddhas, more female gurus, to serve as light bearers and birth workers now. So, if you're hearing this call, join our house or start your own.

To join House of the Leopard, divination is the first step. Through divination we can sit for a one on one consultation to see which Orishas/Neteru are at play in your life then map a process for destiny fulfillment. Initiation can take months or years depending on your commitment to the process.

The greatest benefits of joining a spiritual house to complete initiation are 1) learning a process which can then be replicated and 2) receiving direct transmission from a bonafide spiritual teacher with God-given spiritual shortcuts.

Being bathed in healing herbal waters based on prized House recipes is such a shortcut. Nature knows the truth… even when we forget. Knowing which natural resources to use and which rivers, rocks and leaves hold asé (spiritual essence/power) to cleanse and strengthen one's Ori is paramount. Nature realigns us to our own inherent nature so it's important to choose a teacher who has been given access and authority by the Great Spirit itself.

For whatever reason, maybe you'd prefer to just start your own house. Maybe I talk too much– that's fair *smiles.* To start your own house, simply gather your sisters together. Have tea, discuss their troubles and offer spiritual solutions. Read holy books and mystic verses. Meditate. Divine with cards or runes or stones or simply go into the silence– whatever the Great Oneness reveals to be your method.

You can meet weekly or bi-weekly, but avoid large gaps. A lot can happen to a sister if she is left unsupported for an entire month. As the circle gains momentum through regularity it will take on a life of its own. The dreams will come. Guidance will manifest. You just keep the ship on course.

In order to guide other sisters through their shadows, untying their mental knots, you'll first need to be well acquainted with your own shadows– *and on the other side of them*. If you're still dealing with baggage it's not a good idea to lead others. But once you're solid, don't hold back. They need you to be there at that intersection when they're choosing between right destiny and madness. There will be boogie men chasing them and screaming children. Husbands and boyfriends and pimps… oh my ;) Your job is just to be a constant, a safe port. As their world shifts and changes around them, as the months go by, you just hold the space. Pass the tissue, teach the mantras and the prayers and the songs. Light the candles. Burn the incense. Chant. What is not of AahUah will fall away.

Priesthood Fundamentals

Clothing:
We wear all white, preferably linen or cotton especially during initial initiation phases. Heads wrapped or covered in a veil. No jewelry. No makeup.

Food:
Vegetarian/Vegan/Plant Based. No alcohol. No intoxicants.

Abstinence:
No sexual activity during initiation.

Prayer:
At the crossroad hours of 9, 12, 3, and 6 whenever awake.

Wisdom Texts:
Some holy text should be carried at all times. Ideally several. Bible, Quran, Husia, Sri Guru Granth Sahib, Prt m Hru, Upanishads, Ifa, Vedas, Mystic poetry: Rumi, Kabir, Mirabai, etc.

Sequestered Lifestyle:
A sister should be home and in prayer or meditation as much as possible. She goes out only when unavoidable, for groceries or other responsibilities. Speech should be restricted to bare minimum, only when necessary. She should avoid touching other people or allowing others to touch her... even friends and family. Bowing of the head gently over clasped prayer hands

helps to minimize offending others as you resist touching. No eye contact with anyone. No socializing. One's focus should be more on God than on the world at this time.

Receiving a Sister Into Our Order

After Ruach has confirmed a sister is being called, she should be advised regarding the nature of our lifestyle then tasked with completing her year in white. Initiation begins when she has professed first level vows of chastity, sincerity, and obedience to AahUah/Ruach and His elect within the House. She must agree to following the protocols of prayer and renunciation, with a commitment to studying the prescribed wisdom texts. Dreams are of supreme importance and should be reported at least bi-weekly to the Mother of the House or the senior priestess assigned to the initiate.

There should be no homelife entanglements which prevent full immersion in our way of life. This year of immersion allows for three months of discernment. During that three month period a sister can decide whether our House and this lifestyle is for her. If so, she breaks ties with her previous home to officially become a Sister. After her first year she becomes an official devotee and ultimately, after the Mother of the House approves, she takes on the title of God's Wife.

Depending on the vocation of the House in question, family may be seen by visitation once monthly, in a room designated for this purpose. If the Sisters have established a family-friendly campus, a mother may have her children live with her on site.

Social media and general cell phone use are prohibited during the discernment period so that an initiate can focus on God without distraction. And even after the probationary year, Sisters are focused more on spiritual devotion and household tasks than on social media or superficial conversation.

A new Sister should take on year one attire: 3-5 yards of white fabric as a wrap skirt ending just beneath her knees + a white shirt with no visible cleavage + white cotton shoulder drape + white head covering scarf or veil. Shoes should be white or tan. Her hair should be natural, as it grows, with no need of outside maintenance. Just by walking in Maat, in holiness, a Sister can save another who has yet to profess vows. "Liberation by seeing" is a large part of our work. Be an example– on campus and off.

After entry, the initiate should not go outside the monastery/kehillah/ile walls except for approved useful purposes, and always escorted for safety. When we do go out it should be evident that we represent the Sisterhood and our House at all times. How a Sister carries herself and where she is seen is a reflection on the God she serves.

Devotion, Sincerity and Obedience

All sisters should follow the liturgy of the hours, Shemsu Ra n Dua, praying according to our tradition several times each day. As we submit to Amun and follow the way of the prophets, holy texts should be read silently or aloud before mantra recitation and silent meditation. Zikr and song form a major component of our worship. Any sister who cannot gladly sing God's names would be asked to leave, lest she contaminate the House with ungratefulness or ill will.

Let it never be forgotten that we are here to serve the Most High, to attain an Exalted Mystic Union with our Lord through self-mastery and devotional love. If a Sister loses sight of our raison d-etre, and her very own calling, let her be reminded by a council of senior priestesses and several of her peers in an informal intervention. If this is unsuccessful, the Sister may be asked to leave via a more formal conclave of senior priestesses. This should never be an abrupt dismissal, rather an eventuality after several firm warnings.

When professing initial vows, the new initiate agrees to be obedient to the Mother of the House, Nebethet, any Prophets, senior priestesses and any initiate higher than her in grade (following any reasonable directives without complaint). In the case of viable complaints, the Mother of the House may convene a council to resolve the issue.

We fast regularly and eat minimally. The Daniel Fast is our baseline, followed by a full fast from food at least once per week. Eating foods which come from the Earth, minimally processed, helps us to maintain good health, peace of mind, and gratitude. In time this aspect of devotion will become second nature to a new Sister. Strict daily adherence to the Daniel Fast is at the discretion of each House Mother, according to the true needs of her daughters. Most important is never missing Ekadasi (also Ramadan & Lent by discretion).

Personal hygiene should be maintained at the highest levels as a devotional act. Sisters must always appear clean and well put together… even during fasting.

Fasting from speech is crucial especially during the first probationary year. During the day, new initiates should speak only when spoken to or when unavoidable. Silent hours should be maintained after 8pm and before 8am.

Adherence to the will of the Holy Spirit & ancestral guidance is pivotal. Throughout one's life as a Sister such guidance only increases, as we demonstrate obedience to what we've been shown. But for a new initiate, heeding this guidance will make or break her discernment. Dreams should be reported regularly and any insights heeded. Ifa should be consulted when necessary.

Appointment of House Mother

Mother of the House is a title which no one asks for, nor is it assigned by any human priesthood… male or female. The position of Aset/Nebethet, like that of a prophet, is bequeathed by AahUah itself. She is recognized by the students who naturally gravitate to her, to learn and to be supported. She is a natural teacher, born with her religion.

Ruach and the ancestors will make their choice clear, bestowing authority and favor on this keeper of the Stool. There are certain elekes, certain amabhayi and certain ritual implements which a Mother of the House would possess. If a sister does not have these, she is not ordained to hold the position. Of course, these items are not discussed publicly, to preserve the integrity of the position. This prevents the disingenuous from flaunting superficial accoutrements with no asé. It would be a detriment for seekers to be fooled by false teachers who claim to have knowledge they do not possess. The only certainty I can provide– the only teachers I can truly vouch for– are those who have come through the training processes of my own house. I know my daughters well, and they know these truths well. I know who has been called and by whom to do what. Any successor to the Stool of our House of the Leopard would be appointed from within via Ruach's will. Sister temples are being established on the same basis.

Shemsu Ra n Dua:

Liturgy of the Hours

9:00 AM - Lord Khepri - Rising/Creator
Morning Mass: Eucharistic Adoration

12:00 Noon - Lord Ra - Sustaining

3:00 PM - Lord Eleggua - Choosing

6:00 PM - Lord Tem - Dissolving

Daily Schedule

- Wake up & wash up
- Brief personal prayers
- Get dressed in appropriate garb (by status)
- Prepare tea or coffee for House Mother
- 9:00 am: Morning Prayer & Reflections
- 10:00 - 11:30 am: Chores
- 12 Noon: Brief prayer & mealtime
- 1:00 pm: Constructive work or study
- 3:00 pm: Group prayer
- 4:00 pm: Quiet time or chores
- 6:00 pm: Evening prayer
- 7:00 pm: Bathing/Preparing for bed

Closing Thoughts

You didn't read this by accident. Whether you're a priestess, a doula, a mystic seeker, an LBGTQ+ person, a parent or a general supporter, it's my hope that this text lends some additional understanding.

Let God do a new thing. He's going to do His new thing anyway, but better and easier if we make way for it.

We've made the institution of marriage an idol. We worship it as immutable and set in stone. But, just as we did with Pomba Gira and Santa Clara, we must meditate on marriage as a deific form, as a yidam or murti full of symbolic meaning...

Male + female = birth/child/replication
Male is representative of spirit/formlessness/air/fire
Female is representative of physicality/form/water/earth

We've followed the male + female earthly model, now God is calling us to apply what we've learned to fulfill His blueprint for a more heavenly model. We're graduating.

Homosexual marriage is, in a sense, an evolution of marriage. Union of apparent opposites is shifting to union in sameness. Yet at the same time, ontologically, union precedes separation so same sex union is echoing an ancient/natal cohesion... Such a union is more approximal to our original state, sans Edenic fall.

Our acceptance of this truth increases in proportion to our comprehension of the nature of reality itself. We must look at it from a place of impartiality.

With the increase in same-sex/rainbow unions, we're experiencing now a union of sameness in the physical plane which is allowing for a true union of opposites between the physical and the spiritual planes.

There is no separation.

We are being led beyond duality. One body of Christ. There is no God but The God. The Owner of Everything Owns Everything.

Our task now, as priestesses, is to establish lighthouses... Places of refuge, temples, meeting houses and what have you where womb bearers and those who support us can gather to focus on this work. Initiation training on a mass scale is needed now. To learn how to initiate others, one must first experience initiation oneself. It's time.

Love, bliss, and truth...
Sebai Sekayi

Subhanallah wabihamdihi

Just for the record, the wordplay and etymological comparisons are for edification and further research. Smashing words and concepts together from alternate theologies, breaking barriers, is a way into the Oneness. But it should be understood that the foundation of this prophetic message is in direct revelation– the dreams, mantras, and epiphanies which AahUat naturally receives as a wife and servant of AahUah.

Any misinterpretation or error is solely a result of my own inadequacies. Wherever I have misspoken, may the truth come to light. Wherever there is confusion, may AahUah bring clarity. May the truth of our mystic union with the Great Oneness quell all misunderstandings.

"In Brahman there is no distinction between Purusha (Spirit) and prakriti (matter), and there is no cause and effect. If Brahman alone is the indivisible Supreme Beatitude, how can one say It is male or female?"
-- Avadhuta Gita VI.12

The Night is telling you
"Worship the Day"
As Shivji points to
Al Rahman.
Ilah
of many forms
and formless
RAM
as life, truth,
…and way

Notes

Notes

Notes